DOLORES COUNTY HIGH SCHOOL

115167

D0883358

Marcovitz, Hal
Teens & sex

306.7 Mar

	DATE DUE		

TEENS

&Sex

HAL MARCOVITZ

THE GALLUP YOUTH SURVEY:
MAJOR ISSUES AND TRENDS

Teens and Alcohol

Teens and Family Issues

Teens and Race

Teens, Religion, and Values

Teens and Sex

Teens and Suicide

TEENS
& Sex

HAL MARCOVITZ

Produced by OTTN Publishing, Stockton, New Jersey

Mason Crest Publishers
370 Reed Road
Broomall, PA 19008
www.masoncrest.com

3 5 7 9 8 6 4

Library of Congress Cataloging-in-Publication Data

Marcovitz, Hal.
  Teens and sex / Hal Marcovitz.
      p. cm. — (The Gallup Youth Survey, major issues and trends)
Summary: Using data from the Gallup Youth Survey and other sources, examines
the issue of teenage sexuality, as well as its potential consequences.
Includes bibliographical references and index.
  ISBN 1-59084-722-9
1. Teenagers—Sexual behavior—Juvenile literature. [1. Youth—Sexual
behavior.] I. Title. II. Series.
HQ27.M36 2004
306.7'0835—dc22
                                        2003013293

Contents

Introduction

By George Gallup

As the United States moves into the new century, there is a vital need for insight into what it means to be a young person in America. Today's teenagers—the so-called "Y Generation"—will be the leaders and shapers of the 21st century. The future direction of the United States is being determined now in their hearts and minds and actions. Yet how much do we as a society know about this important segment of the U.S. populace who have the potential to lift our nation to new levels of achievement and social health?

The nation's teen population will top 30 million by the year 2006, the highest number since 1975. Most of these teens will grow up to be responsible citizens and leaders. But some youths face very long odds against reaching adulthood physically safe, behaviorally sound, and economically self-supporting. The challenges presented to society by the less fortunate youth are enormous. To help meet these challenges it is essential to have an accurate picture of the present status of teenagers.

The Gallup Youth Survey—the oldest continuing survey of teenagers—exists to help society meet its responsibility to youth, as well as to inform and guide our leaders by probing the social and economic attitudes and behaviors of young people. With theories abounding about the views, lifestyles, and values of adolescents, the Gallup Youth Survey, through regular scientific measurements of teen themselves, serves as a sort of reality check.

We need to hear more clearly the voices of young people, and to help them better articulate their fears and their hopes. Our youth have much to share with their elders—is the older generation really listening? Is it carefully monitoring the hopes and fears of teenagers today? Failure to do so could result in severe social consequences.

Surveys reveal that the image of teens in the United States today is a negative one. Teens are frequently maligned, misunderstood, or simply ignored by their elders. Yet two decades of the Gallup Youth Survey have provided ample evidence of the very special qualities of the nation's youngsters. In fact, if our society is less racist, less sexist, less polluted, and more peace loving, we can in considerable measure thank our young people, who have been on the leading edge on these issues.

And the younger generation is not geared to greed: survey after survey has shown that teens have a keen interest in helping those people, especially in their own communities, who are less fortunate than themselves

Young people tell the Gallup Youth Survey that they are enthusiastic about helping others, and are willing to work for world peace and a healthy world. They feel positive about their schools and even more positive about their teachers. A large majority of American teenagers report that they are happy and excited about the future, feel very close to their families, are likely to marry, want to have children, are satisfied with their personal lives, and desire to reach the top of their chosen careers.

But young adults face many threats, so parents, guardians, and concerned adults must commit themselves to do everything possible to help tomorrow's parents, citizens, and leaders avoid or overcome risky behaviors so that they can move into the future with greater hope and understanding.

The Gallup Organization and the Gallup Youth Survey are enthusiastic about this partnership with Mason Crest Publishers. Through carefully and clearly written books on a variety of vital topics dealing with teens, Gallup Youth Survey statistics are presented in a way that gives new depth and meaning to the data. The focus of these books is a practical one—to provide readers with the statistics and solid information that they need to understand and to deal with each important topic.

* * *

Schools, churches, and parents are not giving enough attention to a problem of epidemic proportions among America's teenagers—promiscuity and risky sexual behavior. *Teens and Sex* is filled with vital statistics and advice, and covers topics such as public attitudes on sexual matters, sexually transmitted diseases, and methods of birth control— including the most effective method, abstinence.

Parents would be wise to encourage their teenage children to read this clearly written book. It could help teens avoid the lasting consequences of poor decisions regarding sex. It is important that parents read this book as well, so that they will understand the dimensions of the problem. *Teens and Sex* could provide an excellent basis for discussions between parent and child.

Teens today are traveling a confusing and uncertain road in dealing with sexual matters. This book provides an eye-opening reality check for all those who parent or work with teenagers, and offers steps to help teens stay on a safe and healthy track.

Chapter One

Although the rate of teen pregnancy in the United States has fallen in recent years, the fact remains that each year nearly a million girls between the ages of 13 and 19 become pregnant.

When Children Have Children

The good news is that the number of pregnancies among teenage girls is declining. In 1990, 60 out of every 1,000 girls between the ages of 13 and 19 in the United States gave birth. By 2000, that number had fallen to 50 out of every 1,000 teenage girls.

The bad news is that some 900,000 teenage girls in the United States become pregnant every year. Each one of them is faced with gut-wrenching options: seeking an abortion, putting their baby up for adoption, or raising the child on their own.

Girls who elect to keep their babies find their lives dramatically changed. At a time when they should be experiencing the excitement and independence of adolescence, they are instead responsible for meeting the demands of an infant. When they would ordinarily be shopping for prom gowns or visiting colleges, they are instead feeding, bathing, and diapering their babies. Many of them are forced to drop out of school.

Consider the case of Briana Kaley, an 18-year-old teenage mother who wrote about her experiences in *Upfront*, a magazine for young readers published by the *New York Times*. "I had just turned 17 and begun my junior year in high school when the pregnancy test came back positive," Briana wrote. "My pregnancy wasn't planned; it just happened. . . . Before my son was born, I thought, 'It won't be as hard as people say. They just eat, sleep, dirty their diapers and sometimes need baths.' But teenage motherhood has meant great sacrifice."

Briana wrote that although she managed to remain in high school, she had to give up her dream of going away to college. Instead, after graduation she planned to attend a community college part time; meanwhile, she needed to work in order to support her baby. As for her spare time, Briana said there simply isn't any. "After I pick up my son at his sitter's, I have to feed him, clean his laundry, do my own chores, and help around the house," she wrote. "Then I have to play with Bradley. He doesn't play by himself yet, so he needs to be entertained. After two hours of entertaining, I can give him his bath. But then he gets hungry again, and what about my supper? After I finish with him, I get to my homework when it's already time to sleep. I don't have spare time, so I can't go out with my friends. On weekends, I work all day. Most of my income goes to raising my son. I don't go out clothes shopping for myself anymore; it's clothes shopping for Bradley."

Certainly, many young girls are able to tough it out; they raise their babies and make something out of their own lives. The truth is, though, that most teenage mothers face years of regret for their decisions to have sex. Their lives are forever changed by the experience, their potential as young adults never realized, they become a burden on their families and society.

Having Sex

It is a clear and undeniable fact that when teenagers have sex, good things don't often happen. For starters, the encounter itself

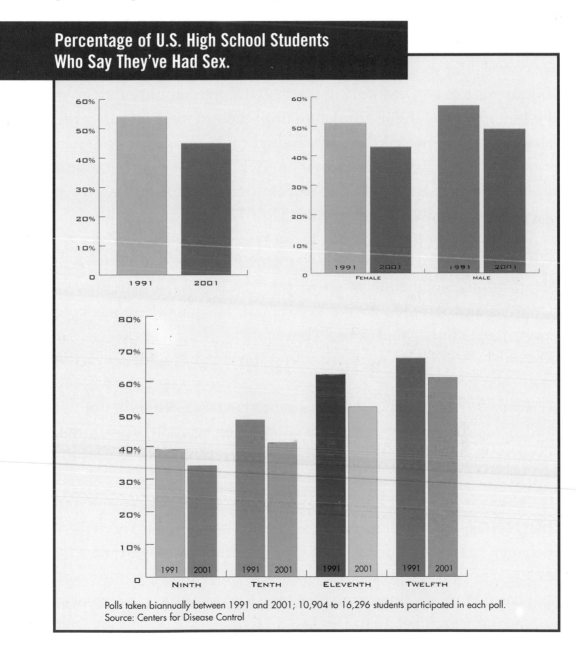

Percentage of U.S. High School Students Who Say They've Had Sex.

Polls taken biannually between 1991 and 2001; 10,904 to 16,296 students participated in each poll.
Source: Centers for Disease Control

rarely involves the tenderness, affection, and intimacy that adults in love usually share. Teenagers are awkward, they don't know what to do, and they are usually in a rush because they have a fear of getting caught.

Actually, that may not be the problem it once was. Years ago, children would never go home to an empty home after school. It was typical for mothers to be at home when the school day ended. If both parents worked during the day, children would often go to the home of a neighbor or relative until their mother or father finished work and picked them up. Today, it is common for both parents to work, and single-parent households have also become more prevalent. As a result, many children are left on their own after school from the time they are 11 or 12 years old.

And what do they do with those hours on their own? A 1992 report published by the Carnegie Council reports that 40 percent of an adolescent's time is spent on "discretionary activities"—activities not devoted to eating, school, homework, household chores, or after-school jobs. Those are a lot of hours to fill. Obviously, some teenagers are filling those hours with sex . . . in their own homes, in their own beds.

Teenagers who make the decision to have sex often do not use contraception. They are at risk of contracting sexually transmitted diseases (STDs), including acquired immune deficiency syndrome (AIDS), which can be fatal.

Teenagers seem to know it's wrong for them to have sex, but then teens often find it fun and exciting to break rules. The typical teenager has a knack for getting into mischief; that is part of adolescence and in most cases it is nothing more than harmless fun that has no long-lasting consequences. However, the consequences of teenage sexual behavior can last a lifetime.

In 2001, the Gallup Organization asked 454 teenagers between the ages of 13 and 17 about activities that would make them feel guilty. This was part of the organization's long-time project tracking the beliefs of young people in the United States, the Gallup Youth Survey. Fifty-nine percent of the respondents admitted that engaging in premarital sex would make them feel guilty. This is a large percentage. However, what was surprising about the results of this Gallup Youth Survey study was that a far larger proportion of the teenagers admitted feelings of guilt for activities with consequences of far less severity than what could happen to them if the condom breaks. For example, 75 percent said they would feel

Many teenagers are unsupervised between the time school lets out and their parents come home from work.

guilty after swearing at a teacher, 77 percent admitted to feelings of guilt for cheating on a test, 81 percent said they would feel guilty if they lied to a friend, and 83 percent said they would feel guilty if they failed to repay a debt.

If a teenager swears at a teacher, he or she could face a detention, which might last for a few hours one afternoon. A pregnancy lasts nine months and often includes many symptoms: the nausea and vomiting that accompany morning sickness; the frequent need to urinate as the fetus presses against the bladder; the enlargement of the mother's breasts as they fill with milk; and the pain of childbirth.

"The baby dropped last week," 15-year-old mother Andrea H. wrote in her Internet journal just a few weeks before she delivered her baby in 1998. "I noticed that my stomach looked different, and after a few tests realized that I no longer suffered from shortness of breath! When the baby moves his head, it feels like someone is twisting my pelvic bone in half, and sometimes I even feel like I'm about to pee in my pants! But I am very glad that this pregnancy is almost over."

As Andrea learned, all mothers-to-be go through physical changes, most of which are not pleasant. In most cases the mother of a planned pregnancy expects those changes and is prepared for them, often not looking at them as an ordeal but as part of the beautiful process of child-bearing. She has mentally prepared herself for the physical demands of pregnancy and can often rely on a dependable support network that includes her husband, physician, childbirth coach, family members, and friends to help her through the rough times.

Adolescents face the same strains on their bodies but with far less of a support network. Research shows they may face other medical issues as well. The National Campaign to Prevent Teen Pregnancy reports that teenage mothers die in childbirth at a rate 2.5 times higher than that of mothers between the ages of 20 and 24. After delivering their babies, teenage mothers are more likely than other women to gain weight or suffer from high blood pres-

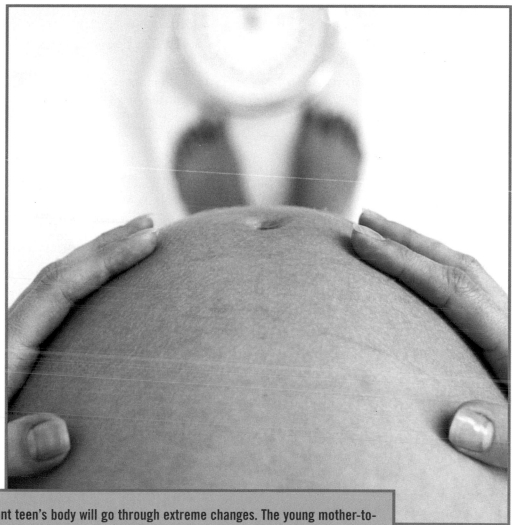

A pregnant teen's body will go through extreme changes. The young mother-to-be must be prepared to deal with the strains on her body. But the greatest changes occur after the baby is born.

sure, anemia, and STDs. Later in life, they tend to be at a greater risk of obesity and the health issues related to being overweight.

Here are more statistics about teens and sex:

It is believed that each year one out of every ten girls between the ages of 15 and 19 will become pregnant.

Thirteen percent of all births in the United States are to teens. About 40 percent of all pregnant teens are age 17 or younger.

Teen pregnancy rates are much higher in the United States than in most other developed countries. The teen pregnancy rate in the United States is twice the rate in Great Britain and Canada, and nine times as high as the rates in the Netherlands and Japan.

Ninety percent of teenagers who have sex practice contraception, although not regularly or correctly. A sexually active teenage girl who does not use contraceptives has a 90 percent chance of becoming pregnant within a year.

A quarter of all teenage mothers have a second child within two years of their first.

Teen Parents

There is no question that the person most affected by a teenage pregnancy is the mother. It is the young mother who must ultimately make the decision about an abortion, an adoption, or whether to raise the baby herself. If she does choose to go through with the pregnancy, it will be her body that will change as the pregnancy proceeds. She will be the one who experiences the pains of labor and delivery. The girls who choose abortion or adoption must come to terms with the psychological issues of terminating the pregnancies or giving up their children to others.

The social implications of teen pregnancy go far beyond whatever may happen to the teenage mother. The National Campaign to Prevent Teen Pregnancy estimates that the bill to U.S. taxpayers for teenage pregnancy runs some $7 billion a year in costs associated with health care, foster care, criminal justice, and welfare payments. Just 41 percent of all teen mothers finish high school. That means they have to accept lower-paying jobs when they finally join the workforce. Nearly half of all teen mothers begin receiving welfare payments within five years of the birth of their children. This means that almost half of the mothers in the United States who had their babies as teens are unable to support themselves and their children on their own and must turn to government assistance programs to help make ends meet.

The fathers usually do not help. Nearly 80 percent of teenage boys who father children do not marry the mothers. The National Campaign to Prevent Teen Pregnancy found that, on average,

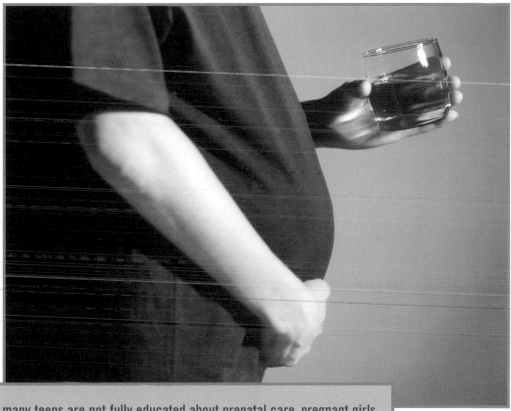

Because many teens are not fully educated about prenatal care, pregnant girls may engage in activities that are harmful to their unborn children, such as drinking alcohol, smoking, or taking drugs.

absentee teenage fathers provide just $800 annually to the support of their children. This just barely covers the cost of diapers for a year.

Some of the fathers do help. They marry the mothers and drop out of school to support their young families. Although these are noble gestures to be sure, very few of those marriages last. Seventy percent of marriages between teen parents end in divorce.

In addition, boys who drop out of school face the same career disadvantages as girls. According to the National Campaign to Prevent Teen Pregnancy, during the past 25 years the median income for college graduates has increased 13 percent, while the

ABSTINENCE

Reports about teenage sexual behavior, and the number of young girls who become pregnant, are common in the media today. What is reported far less, though, is that many teenagers do abstain from sex. They are mature enough to know that sex can lead to pregnancy or disease, and that there are too many opportunities awaiting them in the future to be encumbered with the responsibilities of parenthood at a young age.

Although approximately 900,000 teenage girls in the United States do get pregnant every year, the teen pregnancy rate is declining. The New York-based Alan Guttmacher Institute, an organization that tracks trends in birth control, reports that among American girls between the ages of 15 and 19, the pregnancy rate dropped from 117 pregnancies per 1,000 girls in 1990 to 93 per 1,000 girls in 1997. The Guttmacher Institute believes that 75 percent of this reduction is due to increased use of contraceptives by teens, with the other 25 percent attributed to a changing attitude by teens, who are waiting to have sex.

According to the CDC, the number of high school students who claimed to have never had sex increased by 10 percent between 1991 and 2001. Health educators have started calling this commitment to abstinence the "Let's Not Trend."

"I don't even want a boyfriend until after college," 18-year-old Latoya Huggins of Paterson, New Jersey, told a reporter in 2002 when explaining why she was abstaining from sex. "Basically, I want a lot out of life. My career choices are going to need a lot of time and effort." And college student Lenee Young comment-

median income for high school dropouts has decreased 30 percent. A 2002 report by the National Campaign to Prevent Teen Pregnancy indicates, "When children have children, their opportunities are diminished right from the start, and the future is often one of poverty."

What happens to the babies born to teen parents? Their disadvantages often begin even before they emerge from the womb. Teen mothers don't often receive proper prenatal care. Because they are frightened or otherwise unsure of what to do, teen mothers may delay telling their parents, their school guidance counselors, or other responsible adults about their conditions until they

ed, "A lot of the guys in high school had already had sex. I knew that would come up, so I'd end all my relationships at the very beginning. . . . I feel that part of me hasn't been triggered yet. Sex is one of those things you can't miss until you have it."

Why the trend toward abstinence? There could be a number of reasons. Teenagers have not been immune to the media reports of the AIDS epidemic that often dominated the news during the 1990s. Also, there is no question that sex education in the schools has long stressed abstinence as truly the best way to prevent teen pregnancies and sexually transmitted diseases. In addition, the federal government has decided to place an even greater emphasis on abstinence education in the schools. In 1998, the federal government spent $100 million on programs that promoted abstinence among teenagers; in 2003, the administration of President George W. Bush planned a significant increase in spending on such programs.

Sarah Brown, head of the National Campaign to Prevent Teen Pregnancy, believes there is only one person responsible for making a commitment to abstinence—the teenager who makes that commitment. "The credit for this record-setting decline in teen pregnancy rates goes to teens themselves who are increasingly making smart decisions about delaying sex and using contraception," said Brown. "At the same time that we welcome these declines, we must face the sober reality that we still have a long way to go—nearly four out of 10 girls get pregnant at least once by age 20. So this morning we celebrate, and this afternoon we get back to work convincing teens that they are not ready to be parents."

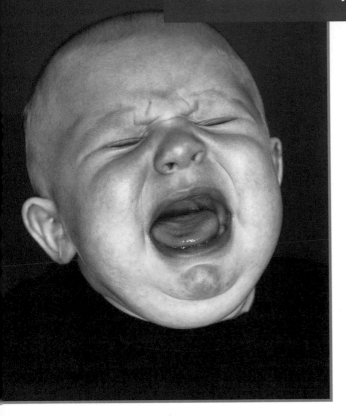

are months into their pregnancies. As a result, they don't eat properly or take the dietary supplements obstetricians typically prescribe during pregnancy. Many pregnant girls don't know that they are not supposed to smoke, take drugs, or drink alcoholic beverages during pregnancy because such substances entering the mother's body can affect the development on the baby.

"No one wants to listen," Andrea H. complained in her journal on February 9, 1998. "Nobody wants to hear how alone I feel or how scared I am. I am absolutely terrified. I don't want to get a doctor's appointment because I don't want to be told I'm pregnant. I mean, I've had zero symptoms except my last period was in November. And if I'm not pregnant, then what the hell is wrong with me? I'm just assuming I am, in which case I have no idea what to do."

Because teens do not typically pursue medical advice early in their pregnancies, the children of teen mothers are more likely to be born prematurely and at a low birth weight, raising the probability of infant death, blindness, deafness, chronic respiratory problems, mental retardation, mental illness, cerebral palsy, dyslexia, and hyperactivity.

Children of teen mothers do worse in school than children born to older parents. They are 50 percent more likely to repeat a grade, are less likely to complete high school than the children of older mothers, and have lower performance scores on standardized tests. The sons of teen mothers are 13 percent more likely to serve time in prison. The daughters of teen parents are 22 percent more likely to become teen mothers themselves.

According to the National Campaign to Prevent Teen Pregnancy, teenagers do not make very good parents. They are simply too young to have mastered the demanding and delicate job of raising children. The children of teen parents also suffer higher rates of abuse and neglect that probably would not occur if their parents had delayed having children. One study showed that 10 percent of incidents involving abuse and neglect of young children occurred in households headed by teen parents. "Few teens are ready for the challenges of parenthood," says Dr. Jeffrey P. Koplan, former director of the U.S. Centers for Disease Control and Prevention (CDC). "When they delay this responsibility it enables them to gain the education and maturity they need to be good parents and good citizens."

Chapter Two

There is only one sure way for teens to avoid pregnancy or sexually transmitted diseases—abstaining from sexual contact. Although abstinence is recommended, teens contemplating sex must talk about their options for protection.

Contraception: No Longer Taboo

There is a scene in the movie *Summer of '42* in which the character Hermie walks into a small-town pharmacy and awkwardly attempts to buy a package of condoms. Hermie and his two friends are 15 years old, and they have decided that the summer of 1942 will be the summer they lose their virginity. At the town drugstore, Hermie fumbles his way through the procurement of prophylactics. Ultimately, he succeeds in obtaining them—after telling the druggist that they will be used as water balloons.

Today, teenagers have far less trouble finding condoms. Pharmacies no longer keep them hidden behind the counter; now they are displayed in the aisles alongside toothbrushes, dental floss, and pain relievers. And teens do not even need to go to the drugstore anymore. A teenager with a credit card can buy them online from any of a number of Internet-based condom merchants.

Buying them is one thing. Using them is another story. According to the CDC's "Youth Risk Behavior Surveillance Report of 2001," just 58 percent of sexually active adolescents reported using condoms during sex. Astonishingly, younger teens were more likely to use condoms than older teens. The report said that 68 percent of sexually active ninth-grade students reported using condoms; 49 percent of sexually active students in the twelfth grade said they used them during sex.

Perhaps the reason for the drop-off in condom use by seniors can be attributed to the availability of birth control pills for older girls. The CDC's report indicated that, overall, 18 percent of teenage girls reported taking birth control pills. Of that number, just 7 percent of sexually active ninth-grade girls reported having birth control prescriptions, while 26 percent of sexually active girls in the twelfth grade said they were taking the "pill." Still, many young people are not practicing any form of birth control.

In 1994, U.S. Surgeon General Jocelyn Elders shocked political conservatives when she advocated distributing condoms in the schools. Such controversial positions eventually led to her dismissal, yet Elders has remained committed to the use of condoms by young people to prevent teenage pregnancies, abortions, and the spread of STDs. A vow of abstinence, Elders insisted, is much easier to break than a latex condom. The government, according to Elders, should "stop worrying about trying to prevent sex and start trying to prevent the consequences of sex."

Contraception has been around in one form or another since approximately 1850 B.C. when Egyptian women fashioned vaginal suppositories out of leaves and honey, which supposedly were effective in blocking sperm. They sometimes added animal dung to the concoction. Five hundred years later, Egyptian men were making prophylactics from papyrus leaves and animal membranes. By the 1500s, prophylactics were made of lamb intestines and fish membranes. By the 1600s, there was reportedly an English physician named "Dr. Condom" who enhanced the development of the modern prophylactic and helped popularize its use. He was honored, so to speak, when users of this new product began referring to them as "condoms."

In the 1700s, the Italian libertine Casanova wrote in his memoirs that he used condoms for both the prevention of unwanted pregnancies and to guard against venereal diseases. In 1843, condom companies started making their products out of rubber; hence giving rise to the slang term "rubbers." Latex replaced rubber in 1930, although the nickname has endured.

In 1861, the *New York Times* published what is believed to have been the first advertisement for condoms. Such ads remained a rarity over the years, appearing mainly in men's magazines. As far as advertising on radio and TV—that was forbidden. In the 1960s, the National Association of

Condoms are available in many places, including men's and women's bathrooms.

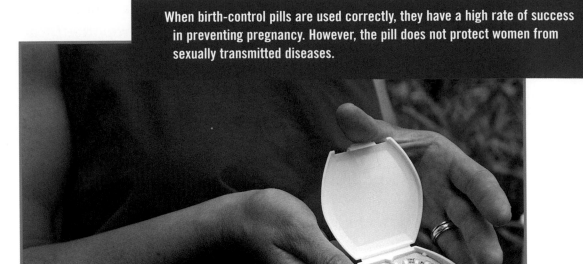

When birth-control pills are used correctly, they have a high rate of success in preventing pregnancy. However, the pill does not protect women from sexually transmitted diseases.

Broadcasters adopted a code of conduct that prohibited condom advertising.

But during the 1980s, the AIDS epidemic became very much of a concern to public health officials. In 1986, Surgeon General Koop endorsed the use of condoms as the only reliable method to prevent the spread of AIDS. Suddenly, condom use had the seal of approval from the federal government. Prophylactics no longer had to be kept behind the counter at the pharmacy. Indeed, the government had declared that people's lives depended on their availability. Condom companies responded by ratcheting up their marketing campaigns.

In 1997 the U.S. Food and Drug Administration (FDA) issued a landmark ruling that cleared the way for prescription drug companies to advertise on television. Quickly, ads promoting prescription drug treatments for stomach pains, asthma, and other ailments hit the airwaves. Eventually, commercials for birth control pills started running on television as well.

Despite the government's promotion of condom use, condom ads remained rare on television networks. In 1985, the ESPN cable network briefly aired condom ads. In 1991, the Fox network aired what was believed to be the first condom ad carried on broadcast television. Throughout this period, network television executives were hesitant to sell time to the condom manufacturers during the prime time hours, the time when most people were likely to be watching their programming. Instead, condom ads were limited to late-night viewing during programming that was adult-oriented—in other words, the networks aired condom ads during times when teenagers were least likely to see them. "We'd prefer to be in prime time but the choice of time is not ours," said Carol Corrozza, vice president of marketing and business development at Ansell LifeStyles, a condom manufacturer. When buying time, she said, "We don't just assume they'll say no. We always try to buy more and let them come back and say no—that's the only way they'll know our intentions."

By 2003, Fox, NBC, and CBS all permitted condom advertising. Cable networks that accept condom ads include Black Entertainment Television (BET), TNT, and CNN, as well as networks with very high concentrations of young viewers, including Comedy Central, E!, MTV, and VH-1.

Teens and Safe Sex

A surgeon general of the United States advised teenagers that they should use condoms. Print advertising for condoms can be found in such teen-oriented publications as *Rolling Stone* and *Spin*, and condom advertisements are becoming more common on television. Even Colin Powell, the much-respected U.S. secretary of state, has urged teens to use prophylactics. "Forget about taboos, forget about conservative ideas with respect to what you should tell young people about," Powell said in a 2002 appearance on MTV. "It's the lives of young people that are put at risk by unsafe sex, and therefore, protect yourself." So why don't most teenagers practice safe sex?

The National Campaign to Prevent Teenage Pregnancy tried to find the answer in 2000 when it conducted a poll of 515 teenagers between the ages of 12 and 17. The study found the vast majority of teenagers—88 percent—agreed it was important to use birth control during sex. However, only 30 percent of teenage girls who participated in the poll said they used birth control the last time they had sex. About 49 percent of the boys and 54 percent of the girls said they did not use birth control because of pressure from their partners. Some 53 percent of the respondents said they did not use birth control because of the effect alcohol or drugs had on their judgment at the time of sex.

Douglas J. Besharov, a scholar at the American Enterprise Institute, a Washington-based organization that examines public policy, says there are many reasons teenagers are reluctant to practice contraception during sex. According to Besharov, one reason is that many Americans, including young people, don't believe it is proper to be prepared for casual sex. He believes that a young man may feel it is rude if, at the moment he has convinced his girlfriend to go all the way, he suddenly produces a condom. "The etiquette of dating is another reason why so many teens do not use contraceptives," says Besharov, who has written extensively on teen pregnancy issues. "Call it the vestiges of Victorian morality or simply good manners, but many Americans do not think it is 'right' to be prepared for casual sex."

As a result, Besharov says, teenagers often find themselves without a method of contraception at the time when they need it the most: "This is a particular problem for teenagers, whose sexual experiences are rarely planned and often sporadic." Finally, though, Besharov points out that teenagers often do not use contraceptives because they simply are not mature enough to make the best decisions: "Teenagers take risks. They experiment with alcohol. They drive fast. They feel they are indestructible. . . . Unprotected sex is just one of a host of dangerous behaviors in which they engage."

A young man unrolls a condom during a demonstration on how to properly use them. Condoms can both prevent pregnancy and the spread of diseases such as AIDS.

Many Methods of Birth Control

Condoms and the pill aren't the only methods of practicing birth control, but they are among the most common methods. Condoms are, for example, available in every drugstore. No prescription is needed. They can also be bought in convenience stories, supermarkets, and over the Internet. Of course, condoms aren't foolproof—there is a danger that a condom can break. Still, they are believed to be up to 98 percent effective in preventing pregnancy and sexually transmitted diseases. As with other methods of birth control, condoms are only at their most effective when the user knows how to use them properly; the condom manufacturers include directions in the boxes, but many people don't bother to read them.

The same latex used in the manufacture of the male condom can be fashioned for female use. Also known as the vaginal pouch, female condoms are 90 percent effective in protecting against pregnancy. They can also protect against the spread of STDs.

The birth control pill requires a doctor's prescription. It is estimated that 100 million women worldwide take oral contraceptives. The pill is regarded as among the most effective contraceptive methods available, with a 99 percent rate of preventing pregnancy.

Instead of taking birth control pills, some women opt for an injectable contraceptive known as Depo-Provera that contains a derivative of the hormone progesterone. The injections must be given every 12 weeks. Women can also use a thin adhesive patch, which is applied to the buttocks, shoulder, upper arm, or abdomen, that slowly releases the hormones progesterone and estrogen into the bloodstream, preventing ovulation. A similar method involves a ring about the size of a silver dollar that is fitted into the vagina, where it releases hormones. All of these methods are believed to be as effective as the birth control pill.

A chemical spermicide called nonoxynol-9 can be obtained in the form of a cream, gel, foam, film, or suppository; it is inserted into the vagina just prior to sex. Nonoxynol-9 neutralizes sperm when it comes into contact with it. Spermicides can be up to 97 percent effective in protecting against pregnancy. Another alternative is a disposable contraceptive sponge, which is inserted into the vagina, covering the cervix; a spermicide in the sponge absorbs sperm.

Two other devices usually used with spermicides are the cervical cap and the diaphragm. The cap, which is made of latex, is inserted into the vagina and placed against the cervix, where it prevents sperm from entering the cervix. The diaphragm is similar, but fashioned in the shape of a cup. Caps and diaphragms are up to 97 percent effective in preventing pregnancy.

There are several birth-control methods that require surgery. Norplant involves a surgical application of six soft capsules underneath the skin of a woman's upper arm, the implants gradually release hormones that prevent ovulation and thicken the barrier the sperm must overcome to pass into the uterus. Norplant lasts up to five years and is believed to be 99 percent effective in preventing pregnancy.

A intrauterine device, or IUD, is a small plastic T-shaped device that is inserted into the uterus; it contains a copper wire, which changes the chemistry of the uterus and destroys sperm. The IUD is up to 99 percent effective in preventing pregnancy.

Two other methods are more permanent, and therefore generally do not apply to teenagers. Tubal ligation is a surgical procedure in which the woman's fallopian tubes, which transport the

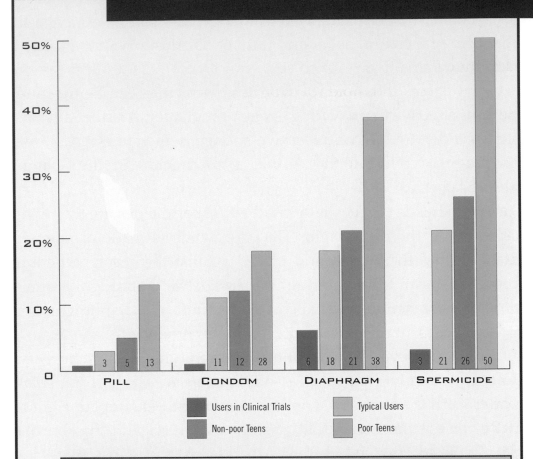

Contraceptive Failure Rates for Different Users

50%

40%

30%

20%

10%

0

PILL	CONDOM	DIAPHRAGM	SPERMICIDE
3 5 13	11 12 28	6 18 21 38	3 21 26 50

Users in Clinical Trials   Typical Users

Non-poor Teens   Poor Teens

The only sure way to prevent pregnancy or the spread of sexually transmitted diseases is abstaining from sex. Although condoms, birth control pills, and other forms of contraception can prevent most unwanted pregnancies, all of these methods can fail. In clinical trials, involving married couples, the typical failure rates are very low: less than 1 percent for the pill, 2 percent for condoms, and 6 percent for the diaphragm. However, studies have shown that the failure rates are higher for typical users—3 percent for the pill, 12 percent for the condom, and 18 percent for the diaphragm. In general, teenagers have higher failure rates than adult users—6 percent for the pill, 13 percent for condoms—while teens from economically disadvantaged families (defined as families with incomes that are 200 percent below the poverty line) had failure rates that are significantly higher—13 percent for the pill, 28 percent for condoms. The rates are much higher even for less effective forms of birth control, such as the diaphragm (38 percent) or spermicides (50 percent).

Sources: *Studies in Family Planning*, vol. 21, no. 1 (Jan/Feb 1990); *Family Planning Perspectives*, vol. 24, no. 1 (Jan/Feb 1992)

eggs from the ovaries to the uterus, are disconnected. A vasectomy is a surgical procedure for men in which the small sperm-carrying tube known as the vas deferens is blocked. This prevents sperm from entering semen. Both tubal ligation and a vasectomy are more than 99 percent effective in preventing pregnancy.

Finally, it is possible for women to take a contraceptive after sex. Sometimes known as the "morning after pill," the emergency contraceptive (EC) treatment is also known as the Yuzpe method, named after its developer, Dr. Albert Yuzpe. The method includes the administration of the hormones estrogen and progestin, which can be effective in blocking ovulation. Taken orally, the pills work up to three days after the sexual encounter. Most states require a prescription to obtain an EC, although they are dispensed in many family planning clinics. ECs are believed to be up to 98 percent effective in preventing pregnancy.

It is important to remember, however, that with the exception of male and female condoms, none of these birth control methods offer any protection against sexually transmitted diseases. Also, the only birth-control method that is guaranteed to prevent pregnancy 100 percent of the time is abstinence. No one who abstains from sex can become pregnant, make his partner pregnant, or become infected with a sexually transmitted disease.

Chapter Three

Protesters hold "Keep Abortion Legal" signs during a pro-choice rally in front of a women's clinic in Buffalo, New York. The issue of abortion was divisive long before the U.S. Supreme Court's landmark *Roe v. Wade* decision made abortion legal in 1973.

Abortion and Adoption: Two Difficult Choices

Teenage girls who get pregnant now have choices as to what to do about their situation. They can choose to have their baby and raise it, have an abortion, or have the baby and surrender custody through adoption. None of these decisions are easy for anyone—let alone a teenager—to make.

Perhaps no subject has divided Americans as much as abortion. It is raised as an issue in most political campaigns. Each Sunday, ministers talk about their opposition to abortion from their pulpits. Physicians who perform abortions have been murdered by extremist anti-abortion rights activists. Abortion clinics have been bombed. Pro-choice advocates can be just as fierce in their support for abortion rights, although they usually don't commit violent acts. Nevertheless, abortion rights advocates are among the most dedicated activists in America, vigorously defending "reproductive rights."

Until relatively recently, abortion had always been a risky medical procedure that often placed the life of the woman in peril. Because of this risk, most states began to forbid abortions as early as the 1820s. By 1900, abortion in America was generally illegal, except in rare cases in which the pregnancy or delivery would place the life of the mother in danger, or if the fetus had been conceived during acts of rape or incest.

But that did not mean there weren't abortions. Women who did not want babies found ways to obtain abortions. Women who had money would go to other countries where abortions were legal, or at least largely overlooked by the government. Women in the United States without money also found ways to obtain them, sometimes from qualified doctors acting in defiance of the law, and sometimes in crude, unhealthy operations performed in less-than-ideal conditions.

The 1960s was an era of great social change in the United States. Feminist groups lobbied for laws that would provide equal employment opportunities for women, including equal pay in the workplace. The idea of reproductive rights was first aired by women who demanded that they have the right to choose whether or not to have a baby. In the meantime, medical procedures had improved. Abortions could now be done safely with little danger to the mother.

In 1973, the U.S. Supreme Court decided the issue in the case *Roe v. Wade* decision. The Court ruled that, within certain limits, a woman had a right to an abortion. According to the Court's decision, states could not pass laws prohibiting an abortion within the first trimester—the first three months—of pregnancy.

In the years following *Roe v. Wade*, abortion opponents have asked the U.S. Supreme Court to reconsider its decision, but the

Court has allowed its 1973 ruling to stand. In recent years, however, lawmakers have struggled over the issue of late-term abortions, known as "partial birth" abortions. Pro-choice advocates believe such abortions should be permitted when there are indications the baby might not survive after birth. Anti-abortion rights advocates argue the fetuses should be protected, and that if late-term abortions were permitted women whose fetuses were normal would ask for the procedure.

Since the *Roe v. Wade* decision, many states have adopted their own laws regulating abortions, particularly with regard to the availability of abortions to teenagers. Forty-three states require

Abortion is a very serious matter. Several states have passed laws that require counseling, parental consent, and a 24-hour waiting period before an abortion procedure is performed.

doctors and abortion clinics to notify parents when a teenage girl requests an abortion. Among the most restrictive states is Pennsylvania. Under that state's Abortion Control Act, a woman who requests an abortion must receive a mandatory counseling session from a physician in which the risks of abortion are spelled out. The woman must then wait 24 hours before the procedure can be performed. Women under the age of 18 must have parental consent; a parent must accompany the girl to the counseling session, then return after 24 hours with the girl and sign a parental consent form.

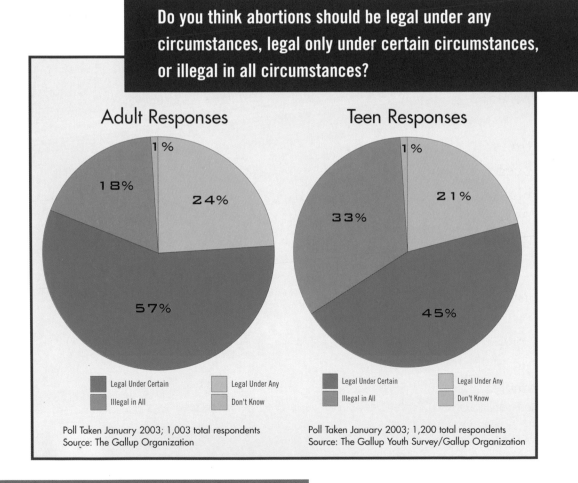

Do you think abortions should be legal under any circumstances, legal only under certain circumstances, or illegal in all circumstances?

Adult Responses

1%
18%
24%
57%

Legal Under Certain   Legal Under Any
Illegal in All   Don't Know

Poll Taken January 2003; 1,003 total respondents
Source: The Gallup Organization

Teen Responses

1%
33%
21%
45%

Legal Under Certain   Legal Under Any
Illegal in All   Don't Know

Poll Taken January 2003; 1,200 total respondents
Source: The Gallup Youth Survey/Gallup Organization

Abortion rights advocates believe that Pennsylvania's law, as well as similar measures in other states, can be harmful to teenage girls because girls are not likely to want to tell their parents they are pregnant. Instead, abortion rights advocates contend, girls might run away from home in search of an abortion in a less-restrictive state, or, perhaps, remain silent about their pregnancies until they are past their first trimester.

States without parental consent laws include Connecticut, Hawaii, New Hampshire, New York, Oregon, Vermont, and Washington. Also, Washington, D.C., does not have a parental consent law. Other states that have consent laws but are far less restrictive than Pennsylvania include Maine, West Virginia, and Maryland; these states permit the physician to waive the consent requirement if he or she believes it is in the best interest of the patient. Another state, Utah, requires the physician to notify the parents "if possible."

Many state legislatures are dominated by opponents of abortion rights. Since 1995, more than 335 anti-abortion measures have been adopted in the country's 50 state legislatures, according to National Abortion and Reproductive Rights Action League (NARAL) Pro-Choice America, one of the nation's largest reproductive rights advocacy groups.

In recent years the abortion rate has declined, particularly among young people. If more teens are using contraception and not getting pregnant, a drop in the abortion rate among young people should be expected. In 2002, the Alan Guttmacher Institute reported that, overall, the abortion rate in the United States declined 11 percent between 1994 and 2000. Among adolescents, the Guttmacher Institute said, the decline was even more significant. The organization reported that between 1994 and 2000, the number of abortions among girls between the ages of 15 and 17 declined by 39 percent, from 24 abortions per 1,000 girls of that age to 15 abortions per 1,000 teenage girls.

What do Teenagers Think?

In 2003, the Gallup Youth Survey asked 1,200 teens between the ages of 13 and 17 to give their views on abortion. The results showed that teenagers are just as divided on the abortion issue as everyone else in America. The survey found that 45 percent of teens thought abortion should be legal under certain circumstances; 21 percent thought abortion should be legal under any circumstances; and 33 percent of the respondents thought abortion should be illegal.

Most abortion rights activists are believed to be women, but the Gallup Youth Survey showed that more teenage boys than girls believe in abortion rights. A total of 35 percent of the girls who responded thought abortion should be illegal, while 32 percent of the boys agreed abortion should be illegal. In addition, 23 percent of the boys and 19 percent of the girls said abortion should be legal under any circumstances.

As for regional views, most teens who believe abortion should be legal live in the Northeast. A total of 74 percent of the respondents in those states thought abortion should be legal under either some or all circumstances. In the West, 71 percent of the teens thought abortion should be legal in some or all circumstances, while in the Midwest, 60 percent of the teenagers shared that view. Finally, in the South, 63 percent of the teenagers who participated in the poll believed abortion should be legal in some or all circumstances.

Although these teens are not old enough to vote, the respondents were asked whether they would vote Democratic,

Republican, or independent when they reach voting age. The Gallup Youth Survey found that 26 percent of future Democrats, 24 percent of future independents, and 14 percent of future Republicans said they believe abortion should be legal under any circumstances. Generally, Democratic political leaders are believed to be more prone to favor abortion rights than are Republican leaders.

Adoption

There is no question that abortion is a difficult decision for most teenage girls. Just as difficult, though, is the decision a girl and her boyfriend may face to give up their baby to adoption. Adoption has its advantages — there are many childless couples in the United States who would be happy to adopt a teenage mother's baby, and no shortage of professional adoption agencies willing to arrange it.

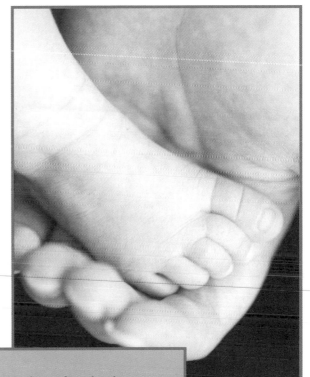

Adoption is an option for teen mothers. However, mothers often develop an emotional connection with their unborn child and have a difficult time parting after the infant is born.

Although there are many childless couples in the United States who would love to adopt, statistics indicate that few teens decide to place their children for adoption. A 1995 survey published in *ChildTrends* found that less than 1 percent of teen mothers choose adoption.

Adoption used to be quite common. When parents learned a teenage daughter was pregnant, they often sent her to live with relatives in a distant city for the duration of her pregnancy. She would have the baby, place it for adoption, and return home to pick up her life as though the pregnancy never occurred.

With the availability of abortion, adoption became the road less traveled for many teenage mothers. And with the rise of women's rights, many young women have chosen to exert their right to keep their baby.

Pregnant teenagers are not unlike older women who become pregnant. They learn to love their babies and form a bond with them while they are still in their wombs. In prior years, the mother who agreed to an adoption never saw the baby again after birth. That has changed. Many young mothers, as well as fathers, can elect for "open adoptions" in which they are given permission to stay in contact with the adoptive parents and the child — under the agreement, though, that they have given up their rights as parents.

All of that takes a lot of planning and forethought — not something that comes easily to most teenagers, particularly during the turbulent time of a pregnancy. As such, few teenage girls choose adoption as an option. Planned Parenthood Federation of America estimates that just 10 percent of babies born to teenage mothers are placed in adoptive homes. Further, Planned Parenthood says, less than 3 percent of pregnant teenage girls make adoption plans before their babies are born, meaning that most decisions about adoption are made at the last minute.

Chapter Four

Many diseases can be passed by sexual contact, and it is rarely obvious that a person is infected. AIDS, for example, is not a disease that exhibits symptoms immediately. Therefore, a person can pass HIV, the virus that causes AIDS, to several partners before realizing he or she is infected.

The Hidden Epidemic

"Not only are teenagers becoming infected with the [AIDS] virus, but it is also being transmitted through heterosexual intercourse, and equal numbers of boys and girls are infected. By contrast, among adults the virus has been transmitted primarily through homosexual sex or intravenous drug use, and the number of infected men far exceeds the number of infected women. Conditions are ripe for the virus to spread because many teenagers have more than one sexual partner and very few use condoms."

This paragraph appeared in a story on the front page of the *New York Times* on October 8, 1989. The story sent shock waves through the ranks of health educators, health professionals, and parents. When AIDS was first detected in the early 1980s, it had been believed that gay men and intravenous drug abusers were the only people at risk; now came the startling news that any young person could get

AIDS and die. Dr. Gary R. Strokash, director of adolescent medicine at Rush Presbyterian St. Luke's Medical Center in Chicago, said then that AIDS among young people "is going to be the next crisis. It's dreadful and it's going to be devastating."

Teens and the Spread of AIDS

Since that news was reported, the spread of AIDS among teenagers has been dreadful but it has not been as devastating as originally projected. Government officials and health educators responded to the crisis. Nearly 90 percent of young people in the United States report receiving information in their health education classes about AIDS and how it is spread. In the meantime, medical research has advanced. While there is still no cure, there are drugs and treatments that extend the lives of people living with the disease. Having AIDS is no longer an automatic death sentence, although it is certainly a life sentence that often includes taking expensive drugs that can have unpleasant and debilitating side effects. Nevertheless, the CDC reports that the death rate for AIDS patients declined by 70 percent between 1995 and 2001.

In 2003, the Gallup Youth Survey asked 1,200 young people their thoughts on the most serious health crises facing Americans. Twenty-four percent of teenagers participating in the poll identified AIDS as the "most urgent health problem facing this country at the present time." Other health concerns raised by young people included cancer (17 percent), obesity (12 percent), the rising cost of health care and insurance (7 percent), heart disease (2 percent), and tobacco-related illnesses (2 percent).

Despite their acknowledgment that AIDS is a serious health issue, teenagers get AIDS and they get lots of other sexually transmitted diseases, too. A 2001 CDC report said, "Compared to older

Young people who decide to have sex must insist on using some form of protection that will prevent the spread of disease in addition to birth control.

adults, adolescents and young adults are at a higher risk for acquiring STDs for a number of reasons: they may be more likely to have multiple sexual partners rather than a single, long-term relationship, and they may select partners at a higher risk." It is estimated that each year, about 3 million teenagers — or one in four sexually active young people — contract an STD. Here are some other statistics compiled by the CDC:

> Women between the ages of 15 and 19 had the highest rate of gonorrhea in 2001, compared with women of all other age groups.
>
> Adolescent girls from poor urban neighborhoods are regarded as highly susceptible to contracting chlamydia. One study conducted among 16 inner-city health organizations found that nearly 10 percent of girls under the age of 20 tested positive for the infection.
>
> In 2000, 1,688 people under the age of 24 contracted AIDS, bringing the cumulative total in that age group to 31,293. Of the 1,688 new cases reported in 2000, 9 percent of the men who contracted the disease became infected through unprotected heterosexual sex; 45 percent of the women who were infected said they believed they contracted the disease through unprotected sex with male partners.

"STDs are hidden epidemics of enormous health and economic consequence in the United States," the CDC report continued. "They are hidden because many Americans are reluctant to address sexual health issues in an open way. . . . All Americans have an interest in STD prevention because all communities are impacted by STDs and all individuals directly or indirectly pay the costs of these diseases."

AIDS and Other STDs

Sex requires personal contact. That means you can catch a cold from your partner during sex. There are few effective ways to guard against catching a cold, but many health professionals argue that if you are not going to abstain from sex, the best way to avoid an STD is to use a condom. If you don't, you may catch one

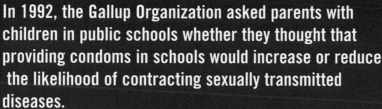

In 1992, the Gallup Organization asked parents with children in public schools whether they thought that providing condoms in schools would increase or reduce the likelihood of contracting sexually transmitted diseases.

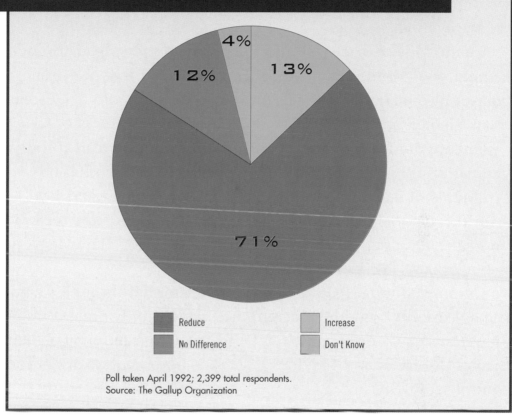

4%

13%

12%

71%

Reduce   Increase

No Difference   Don't Know

Poll taken April 1992; 2,399 total respondents.
Source: The Gallup Organization

of these STDs—all of which are a lot more unpleasant than a cold. With the exception of AIDS, most are rarely fatal unless they are ignored, and most can either be treated or cured with medications.

AIDS and HIV. The virus that causes AIDS is HIV, or human immunodeficiency virus. HIV can lie dormant in the body for years before it becomes active, weakening the body's immune system, making it hard for the victim to fight off infections and other diseases that occur because of the weakened immune system. AIDS is the final stage of the disease. The virus is spread through blood, semen, vaginal secretions, and breast milk; transmission occurs when one of those fluids comes into contact with an open cut or sore, or one of the mucous membranes in the vagina, penis, rectum, or mouth. The virus can also be transmitted through sharing intravenous needles.

Chancroids. A bacterial infection, chancroids spread through vaginal, anal, or oral intercourse. Those infected will notice small boils or ulcers on their genitals that could develop into open sores or swollen glands.

Chlamydia trachomatis. A bacterial infection spread through vaginal or anal intercourse, chlamydia trachomatis often has no symptoms. It can cause sterility in men and women and lead to arthritis, bladder infections, pelvic inflammation, and ectopic pregnancy (a pregnancy in which the fertilized egg plants itself in the fallopian tube).

Cytomegalovirus (CMV). CMV is transmitted through saliva, semen, blood, vaginal secretions, urine, and breast milk. Symptoms show up mostly in infants; those infected may exhibit mental disorders and blindness. There is no cure, but drugs can control symptoms.

Gonorrhea. One of the oldest known sexually transmitted diseases, gonorrhea, if left untreated, can cause sterility, arthritis, heart problems, nervous disorders, stillbirth, and premature labor. It is easily treatable with antibiotics.

Hepatitis B (HBV). The virus HBV can be spread through sexual contact and intravenous drug use. It can cause liver disease and death. Vaccinations are available and symptoms can be treated, but it has no cure.

Herpes. Herpes simplex virus, or HSV, comes in two varieties: HSV type-1 causes cold sores; type-2 generally affects the genitals, causing recurring and often itchy and painful rashes and blisters. Symptoms can be treated, but there is no cure and the virus often manifests itself from time to time over the person's lifetime.

CHLAMYDIA

Chlamydia trachomatis is the most prevalent sexually transmitted disease in the United States today. Nearly 800,000 cases were reported to the Centers for Disease Control in 2001. It is estimated that there are 278 cases for every 100,000 people in the United States. Women are four times as likely as men to contract chlamydia.

For adolescents, the rates have been growing in recent years. In 1997, the CDC reported that 194,256 girls between the ages of 15 and 19 and 24,032 boys in that age group had contracted chlamydia. In 2001, those numbers grew to 249,269 girls and 39,064 boys.

Often, symptoms do not occur in girls, and are so fast to occur in boys that they often don't realize they have them, or they believe they are caused by some other illness. When symptoms do occur in girls, they include bleeding between periods, vaginal bleeding after intercourse, abdominal pain, painful intercourse, fever, frequent urge to urinate, inflammation of the cervix, and abnormal vaginal discharge. Symptoms in boys include a watery or milky discharge from the penis, swollen or tender testicles, and pain or burning sensation during urination.

In girls, untreated chlamydia may infect the cervix and then spread to the fallopian tubes or ovaries, causing pelvic inflammatory disease (PID). That can lead to sterility or an ectopic pregnancy, which can be fatal if the pregnancy progresses to the point where the tube bursts. Men can suffer sterilization from chlamydia as well; if the infection spreads from the urethra to the testicles, a condition known as epididymitis could develop. Epididymitis can lead to sterility. Men can also develop Reiter's syndrome if chlamydia is left untreated. Reiter's syndrome can cause arthritis.

Chlamydia is easy to diagnose—usually through a cervical exam and urine test, and can be treated with antibiotics.

Human papillomavirus (HPV). HPV is a group of 60 viruses that cause genital warts. It is spread through vaginal and anal intercourse.

Molluscum contagiosum. A virus spread through vaginal, anal and oral intercourse, molluscum causes pimples on the genitals and thighs.

Syphilis. Another of the oldest known STDs, syphilis is spread through intimate contact. The bacteria can cause damage to the heart, brain, and nervous system and can lead to death. Infamous

AIDS: A BRIEF HISTORY

Medical researchers believe that AIDS was a disease confined to chimpanzees in Africa until it spread from apes to humans. In 1959, a man died in the Congo in what researchers believe was the first human death caused by AIDS.

In 1978, gay men in the United States and Sweden and heterosexuals in Haiti and Tanzania started showing symptoms of decreased immunities. By 1980, 31 gay men in the United States had died of the mysterious illness. A year later, the CDC reported an alarming increase in the number of otherwise healthy gay men who had contracted a form of cancer known as Kaposi's sarcoma. At first, the CDC called the epidemic GRID—gay-related immune deficiency. The government agency reported that 422 cases of GRID had been diagnosed in the United States, causing 159 deaths.

The death toll rose to 619 in 1982 and 2,122 in 1983. Medical researchers now started calling the disease AIDS. That year, the French medical research organization Instiut Pasteur discovered the link between AIDS and HIV. By 1984, some 11,000 AIDS cases had been diagnosed; the death toll that year was reported at 5,620.

By then, AIDS was becoming something of a plague on celebrities. Movie star Rock Hudson, who led a secret gay life despite his reputation as a leading man in many Hollywood movies, died of AIDS in 1985. Other celebrities who would die from AIDS included fashion

mobster Al Capone died from untreated syphilis—after he went insane. However, the disease can be treated with common antibiotics.

Although condoms can prevent the transmission of many sexually transmitted diseases, even when teenagers use them for vaginal intercourse they still find other ways of contracting diseases. In 1999, the *Washington Post* reported an "unsettling new fad" among middle-class suburban teenagers. The newspaper

designer Halston, actor Robert Reed, and ballet dancer Rudolf Nureyev. Tennis pro Arthur Ashe died of AIDS; his death was attributed to a tainted blood transfusion. Basketball star Magic Johnson was diagnosed with HIV and forced to retire prematurely from the NBA; he has survived.

In 1986, Surgeon General C. Everett Koop declared that condoms were the only effective way to prevent the spread of AIDS. By 1988, more than 100 million copies of Koop's booklet, Understanding AIDS, had been published and distributed by the federal government. That year, the death toll in the United States was reported at 62,101 people. The following year, health officials announced that teenagers were at risk.

Medical advances started bearing fruit in the 1990s. A variety of drugs that had been in development since the epidemic was first reported were by then winning approval from the FDA. The drugs were not inoculations or cures, but they did stall the progression of the disease as well as help people living with HIV and AIDS to recover and fight off the infections and diseases that attack the body in its immune-weakened state.

Research continues, but sadly the death toll in the United States has continued to rise, although there is no question that AIDS deaths have declined in recent years. In 2000, the total AIDS death toll in the United States passed 400,000. Other parts of the world, particularly underdeveloped countries in Asia and Africa, have been hit much harder by the disease. Internationally, it is believed that more than 6 million people have died of AIDS.

A person diagnosed with a sexually transmitted disease has a responsibility to inform his or her partner before engaging in intimate contact.

reported that young people, fearful of STDs and pregnancy, were instead turning to oral sex as an alternative to vaginal intercourse. A year later, the *New York Times* interviewed a number of seventh- and eighth-grade students; one girl told the newspaper that performing oral sex on her boyfriends was like giving "a goodnight kiss to them." It is doubtful that those girls were making their boyfriends unroll condoms beforehand.

Chapter Five

Every day, teens in the United States are inundated with sexual messages in movies, television, music, and other media.

Going Too Far

In the United States, teenagers buy the most compact discs. They go to the movies more often than adults. They spend the most hours watching TV. They play video and computer games more than people of other ages. And through it all, they are constantly bombarded with sexually suggestive music and images.

There have been many studies of the influence of the entertainment media on young people's sexual habits, and practically all have concluded that teenagers are led to believe sex is permissible because it is portrayed so often in the movies and television programs they watch. Mediascope, a California-based media watchdog group that monitors the content of movies and television programming, recently issued the results of a study in which three out of four teens reported that "TV shows and movies make it seem normal for teenagers to have sex." Mediascope also reported that 63 percent of entertainment industry executives who took part in a survey felt that television's portrayal of sex influences young people's decisions to have sex. Mediascope's findings include:

> Teenagers between the age of 13 and 15 rank the entertainment media as the top source of their information about sexuality and sexual health.
>
> Half of the teenagers said they have learned "a lot" about pregnancy and birth control from TV shows and movies.
>
> Four out of 10 teenagers said they have gotten ideas from the entertainment media about how to talk to their boyfriends or girlfriends about sexual issues.
>
> Teenagers are exposed to some 14,000 references to sex a year on television.
>
> Seventy-five percent of all television programs include some degree of sexual content. It is possible to see nearly six scenes an hour on television that contain sexual behavior or sexually suggestive dialogue.

Although there are an abundant number of sexual images on television, they are rarely balanced with messages about avoiding unwanted pregnancies, protecting against sexually transmitted diseases, or examinations of the basic question of whether sex among adolescents is a good idea in the first place. Mediascope determined that just 4 percent of sexually oriented scenes on television alluded to the risks and responsibilities of sex. "These infrequent portrayals of sexual risks such as disease and pregnancy trivialize the importance of sexual responsibility and can give teenagers an unrealistic view of precautions they should take," the Mediascope report said. "Furthermore, without reinforcing the idea of cautionary behavior before every sexual encounter, the importance of sexual responsibility and consistent contraceptive use is completely undermined."

Music

Mediascope also found that the music industry was becoming more sexually explicit. Music has long relied on sexual undertones; after all, most songs are about relationships between young lovers. For decades, though, the sex in music was for the most part implied. Artists and producers were very careful not to cross the threshold. In 1956, when Elvis Presley first appeared on the *Ed Sullivan Show*, television censors were appalled when the singer swiveled his hips; in subsequent appearances, cameramen were ordered to shoot Elvis from the waist up.

Beginning in the 1980s, though, sexual references in songs became less implied and more direct. Mediascope reports, "The amount of sexual references did not drastically increase, but the language used to describe sexual behavior became more graphic."

The 1980s was also the decade in which music videos became an important and influential part of the

Teens are often exposed to sexually explicit lyrics in popular music. Since 1985, record companies have placed warning labels on albums that contain songs with sexual or violent themes.

recording industry. Suddenly, artists were adding pictures to their words. It didn't take long for the videos to become sexually suggestive. Madonna, whose first big hit was titled "Like a Virgin," became a superstar. To illustrate just how much Madonna relied on her image as a sexually active woman to sell her music, the singer appeared, mostly in the nude, in a 1992 book of photographs that was appropriately titled *Sex*.

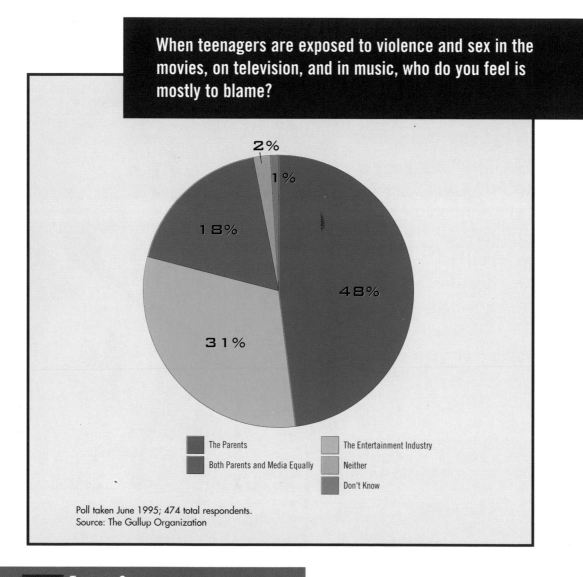

When teenagers are exposed to violence and sex in the movies, on television, and in music, who do you feel is mostly to blame?

2%
1%
18%
48%
31%

The Parents
Both Parents and Media Equally
The Entertainment Industry
Neither
Don't Know

Poll taken June 1995; 474 total respondents.
Source: The Gallup Organization

Movies

Movies routinely simulate sex on screen, but for years film producers were able to argue that young audiences were shielded from the more graphic images through the industry's self-rating system. In the 1980s, director John Hughes produced a number of teen-oriented movies, such as *The Breakfast Club* and *Sixteen Candles*, that showed teenagers suffering from the pressures, angst, and alienation that many adults experience. The Hughes films also suggested that teenagers have sex—just like adults do.

The Hughes films were highly praised; critics declared that Hughes had made a connection with young people and showed what life as a teenager was really like. Other directors were quick to copy Hughes. Although many of them sought to portray teen life, what most of them ultimately portrayed was simply teen sex. By the late 1990s, such films as *American Pie* and *Go* were raking in millions of dollars at the suburban multiplexes. Even such long-time entertainment pros as Aaron Spelling could not believe what they were seeing on the screen. "I abhor some of these teenage movies," said Spelling, the producer of the television show *Beverly Hills 90210*, which frequently and unabashedly featured plots that suggested teen sex. "I think they're going too far. If they're going to have sexual affairs, I like to see condoms. We do it on TV. I think they should do it."

Television

There is no question that television often goes too far as well. The media watchdog group Parents Television Council has noted the sexual content of some popular television shows aired over the past few years that are aimed directly at adolescents, such as *Dawson's Creek*, *Buffy the Vampire Slayer*, *Angel*, *Charmed*, and

The Internet is another medium that can convey sexual images to teenagers. This has forced schools, libraries, and other public places where Internet access is offered to filter the content young people can view on the Web.

Sabrina the Teenage Witch. Of the very popular *Buffy the Vampire Slayer*, Parents Television Council said the "pervasive and graphic sexual content has been considerably toned down . . . but inappropriate and crude sexual references do remain. Therefore, the rating for sexual content on this show remains 'red.'" The PTC commented, "This series is not appropriate for young children or adolescents." The organization also denounced *Sabrina the Teenage Witch*, once one of television's most wholesome shows and one aimed particularly at young adolescent girls. The Parents Television Council wrote, "Unfortunately, in an attempt to reflect the principal character's maturation, 'Sabrina' has introduced elements that would be inappropriate or unexpected for a show targeting a pre-teen and early teen audience."

Desensitization

The result of inundating young people with hours and hours of sexual content in their entertainment is obvious. They have become desensitized, and do not appreciate sexual content for what it truly is. The Gallup Youth Survey has been examining the issue of sex in the media for years. The findings are startling, for they show that teenagers have been desensitized to sex but do not realize it.

In 1977, when The Gallup Organization asked 502 U.S. teenagers between the ages of 13 and 17 whether they felt there was too much sex in the movies, 44 percent said yes. In 1999, The Gallup Organization asked the same question of another 502 teenagers. This time, 28 percent of the respondents said they thought movies included too much sex.

What happened during the 22 years between surveys? Teenagers were inundated with thousands and thousands of hours of sex in the movies and on the television screen. Someone who grows up in a world of dramatized or virtual sex may not find a steady diet of sex acts on the multiplex screen to be all that unusual. "Young people tell me that the media is one of their leading sources of information about sex," says Dr. Michael Rich, a pediatrician who testified before Congress on the issue of sex in the media. "Each year, television and the movies offer 14,000 sexual portrayals, of which only 165 deal with risks of pregnancy, HIV, or other sexually transmitted diseases. It seems unrealistic that society should place the sole blame on our young people for

critics went beyond the law. In 1968, prints of the Swedish art film *I Am Curious Yellow* were seized by U.S. Customs agents before they could be distributed to American theaters. The Customs Service alleged the movie's stark depictions of nudity and sex were obscene. A federal jury agreed with the ban, but the decision was overturned on appeal and the film was eventually shown in U.S. theaters — to standing-room-only audiences, of course.

In any event, American filmmakers knew they would have to develop guidelines or face similar court challenges to their work. In 1968, motion picture industry executives developed a film rating system that included the designations "G" for general audiences, "M" for mature, "R" for restricted to viewers over the age of 17 unless accompanied by an adult, and "X" for no one under 17 admitted at all. Over the years, the ratings have undergone several adjustments. The ratings now include "G" as well as "PG" for parental guidance advised, "PG-13" for no admission under the age of 13 without an adult, "R," and "NC-17," which largely replaced the "X" rating. In addition, films rated "R" carry warning information advising viewers that the content of the movie may include violence, sex, drug use, or other mature content.

The ratings are applied to films by a review board established by the Motion Picture Association of America (MPAA). There are appeals processes for the filmmaker who doesn't agree with the film's ratings. Filmmakers are under no requirement to submit the films to the MPAA ratings board, but most do because studios that finance the films usually demand it to comply with public sensitivities.

Other entertainment media have been slow to copy the ratings system employed by the film industry, but most sectors of the entertainment business eventually found a way to balance the public's desire for responsibility against the constitutional guarantee that artists should be permitted to work in an uncensored environment.

The music industry started placing warning labels to recordings in 1985, advising listeners that the lyrics contained descriptions of violence and sex.

The video game industry had also adopted a rating system to help guide buyers and advise parents to the nature of the content contained in games. The rating system includes "EC," for games appropriate for players 3 years old and older; "E" for everyone, which means the content is suitable for anyone, although players

The makers of video games have developed a rating system to help parents determine whether a particular game is suitable for their children.

Chapter Six

Although many teenagers say that gays and lesbians should be treated no differently than other people, gay teens often feel isolated from their classmates.

Attempting to Become Invisible

In 2001, Dominick Halse, a 16-year-old gay high school student from Castleton on Hudson, New York, told a reporter that he spends his days in school avoiding physical and verbal abuse from his classmates. "There are boys who said they would like to kill me and drag me behind a car, or take me to an island with all the other gays and shoot me," Halse said. "You don't need death threats as a child."

Another gay student, Jesse Fuenes, had this to say about her experiences at a California high school: "I had pebbles thrown at me for a week and a half. That ended up in rock throwing and I was bleeding."

According to the organization Human Rights Watch, such experiences by gay students are typical. The organization released a report in 2001 that said the nation's 2 million gay high school students are constantly threatened and abused, and many often attend classes in fear of their lives: "These students spend an inordinate amount of energy figuring out how to get to and from school safely, avoiding the hallways when other students are present in order to escape slurs and shoves, cutting gym class to escape being beaten up—in short, attempting to become invisible."

Changing Times, Changing Attitudes

Adolescence can be a confusing and awkward time for many teens as they undergo changes in their bodies, learn about dating, and experience their first relationships. Teenagers who believe they are gay not only face these pressures, they must also come to terms with their sexuality. And they must come to terms with their sexuality during a time in which many gay adults feel empowered to be honest and public about themselves. Years ago, few gay people publicly acknowledged their sexual preferences, preferring instead to keep their orientation a secret to all except others in the gay community. That has changed. Gay people march in gay rights parades. They publish their own newspapers and magazines. They pressure state legislatures and city governments to adopt laws defining their rights as citizens.

Gay teenagers also feel the need to be honest about their sexuality to themselves and others. According to Human Rights Watch, "youths are 'coming out'—identifying themselves as gay, lesbian, bisexual, or transgender . . . at younger ages." The organization reported that according to studies, girls have reported recognizing that they are lesbians at ages as young as 10 and have their first same-sex experience at the age of 15. Meanwhile, boys report finding themselves attracted to other boys at ages as young as 9 and have said that their first same-sex experiences occurred at ages as young as 13.

In society, most adults have learned to accept gays and lesbians as coworkers and recognize their rights. The Gallup Organization found that many young people are also willing to accept gays and acknowledge their rights. In 1998, the Gallup Youth Survey found that most young people support equal rights for gays. In its survey of 500 teens, 82 percent said gays should be treated equally in the workplace, and 80 percent said health benefits should be extended to the partners of gay employees. A total of 73 percent said gays should have the right to join the armed forces; 64 percent thought they should be able to adopt children.

And yet, young gays are still made to feel like outcasts. The Washington-based National Gay and Lesbian Task Force estimated that by the late 1990s, no fewer than 49 proposals to deny rights to gays and lesbians were making their way through state legislatures. Eighteen states sought to ban gay marriages. Some of the legislative efforts were aimed directly at gay teens. For example, Utah took the dramatic step of barring all extracurricular clubs at schools rather than permit alliances of gay and lesbian students to meet on school grounds. In 1999, anti-gay groups in Oregon circulated petitions seeking to bar discussion of gay and lesbian issues in classrooms.

Gay rights advocates believe such measures are sponsored by a vocal minority of lawmakers who, nevertheless, hold a considerable amount of influence in their state capitals. There is also a vocal and hateful minority of young people who dominate their school environments, making life difficult and dangerous for gay students. Human Rights Watch reported, "Although some lesbian, gay, bisexual and transgender students in the United States experience a positive, welcoming environment at school, the vast majority are not so fortunate. Lesbian, gay and bisexual youth are nearly three times as likely as their heterosexual peers to have been assaulted or involved in at least one physical fight in school, three times as likely to have been threatened or injured with a weapon at school, and nearly four times as likely to skip school because they felt unsafe."

With gay students facing such mental anguish, it is not surprising that a New York University School of Medicine study found a high rate of attempted suicide in the teenage gay community. The 2001 study of New York state teens found that 28 percent of gay males and 21 percent of gay females in the seventh through twelfth grades had reported attempting suicide.

A separate study conducted in 1989 by the U.S. Alcohol, Drug Abuse, and Mental Health Administration also reported a high suicide rate among gay teens, finding that young gay and lesbian people are confused and traumatized by society's attitudes toward homosexuality. "No group of people are more strongly affected by the attitudes and conduct of society than are the young," said the study. "Gay and lesbian youth are strongly affected by the negative attitudes and hostile responses of society to homosexuality. The resulting poor self-esteem, depression, and fear can be a fatal blow to a fragile identity."

Gay rights advocates as well as others see a direct connection between discrimination against gays and the suicide rate among gay and lesbian young people. "This issue is not about a 'different' way of life; it is about life itself," said former Massachusetts Governor William Weld. "I know that every teacher and every parent . . . fundamentally agrees that no young person—gay or straight—should be driven to take his or her life because of isolation and abuse. This is a tragedy we must all work together to prevent. We can take the first step toward ending gay youth suicide by creating an atmosphere of dignity and respect for these young people in our schools."

Gay Teens and STDs

Gay teenagers face more than just discrimination or mental and physical abuse from their classmates. They face the same dangers from sexually transmitted diseases that are faced by heterosexual teenagers. "Like other teens, many young men who have sex with men experience a phase of sexual experimentation marked by multiple sexual partners," said a report issued by Advocates for Youth, a Washington-based organization that promotes safe sex by young people. "Human immunodeficiency virus and sexually transmitted disease risk increases with the number of sexual partners, and, in one study, 43.6 percent of surveyed young [gay] men reported at least 10 sexual partners."

The Advocates for Youth report argued that sex education programs in schools are not geared toward alerting gay teenagers to the dangers of STDs, but are instead structured to provide information to heterosexual students. As a result, the report said, the messages contained in high school sex education classes may not be connecting with gay students. For example, the report said, many older gay men have been a part of the homosexual culture since the AIDS virus first spread and became an epidemic in the 1980s. Chances are, those men lost friends to AIDS. As a result, the danger of AIDS is very real to them, and they have learned through the mistakes of others to protect themselves when having sex.

Younger gay males have come of age during a time when the AIDS death rate has been reduced and drugs have been developed that are affective in helping the body fight off infections caused by a weakened immune system. To them, the threat of

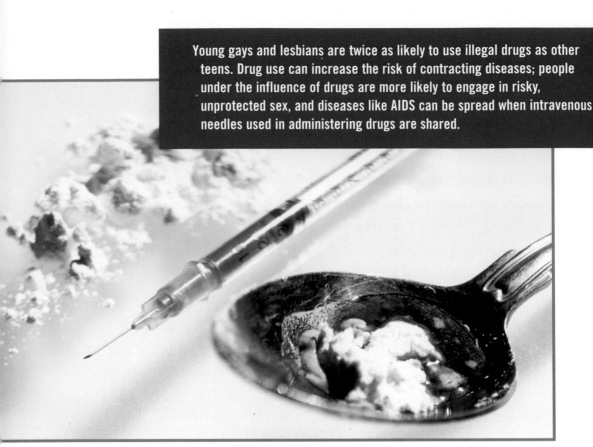

Young gays and lesbians are twice as likely to use illegal drugs as other teens. Drug use can increase the risk of contracting diseases; people under the influence of drugs are more likely to engage in risky, unprotected sex, and diseases like AIDS can be spread when intravenous needles used in administering drugs are shared.

AIDS is much less scary. "Few young men who have sex with men today have witnessed the deadly consequences of unsafe behavior, and many do not feel particularly susceptible to HIV," the Advocates for Youth report said. "Some young [gays] may associate HIV with older gay men and assume young, apparently healthy partners are HIV-negative. . . . Perceived invulnerability is characteristic of youth but is problematic for young men who have sex with men, considering their risk for HIV and their lower rates of safer sex as compared to older gay males."

Advocates for Youth also contended that when gay teenagers feel threatened by their classmates, they have few places to go for counseling or social support. Instead, they turn to drugs and alcohol. The organization found that young gays and lesbians are twice as likely as other people to use alcohol, three times as likely as others to use marijuana, and eight times as likely as others to use cocaine. What happens when somebody has had too much to drink or is under the influence of drugs and alcohol? "Drug or alcohol use may make negotiating safer sex more difficult and increase the likelihood of unprotected sex," the Advocates for Youth report said.

The Advocates for Youth study contained a statement from Pedro Zamora, an AIDS patient featured on the MTV television program *The Real World*, who died in 1994 at the age of 22. Before he died, Zamora said, "I needed positive messages about my sexuality. I needed to know about condoms, how to use them correctly and where to buy them. I needed to know that you could be sexual without having intercourse. I needed to know how to say, 'I don't want to have intercourse, I just want to be held.'"

In 2000 the Centers for Disease Control released the results of a study involving 2,621 gay and bisexual men between the ages of 15 and 25. According to the CDC report, 22 percent had never been tested for HIV. Additionally, half of the participants had not been tested within six months of the study. This means that some 1,300 of these young gay men may have been carrying HIV but were not aware of it.

In a separate study of 3,492 gay and bisexual men between the ages of 15 and 22, the CDC found that 25 percent of the participants reported having unprotected sex with both men and women. "The study confirms that young bisexual men are a 'bridge' for HIV transmission to women, particularly since 6.6 percent of the bisexual men in the study were HIV positive," reported the CDC.

Chapter Seven

Many girls who are rape victims experience guilt, as if they had contributed to the incident in some way. However, this feeling is wrong: rape is a violent crime.

Hidden Rape

Christy and her friend Hope had gone to an off-campus party, had a few beers, and were on their way back to their dormitory rooms at a college in Virginia when they heard whistles from above. Two male students were leaning out of a third-floor dorm window. The boys invited Christy and Hope up to their room for a nightcap. Since they were in a party mood, the girls decided to take the boys up on their offer.

"So we just go up," Christy recalled later. "We're going up to Hope's room, which is on the same floor, and we decided to drop in on these guys, just to say hello, nothing more. We go down the hall and they say, 'Oh, I'm so-and-so and so-and-so, and we're football players.' I almost cracked up, because I was a jock in high school so it didn't impress me."

After a few minutes, though, things began going terribly wrong for the two girls. It soon became clear the two boys wanted to have sex with the girls. Neither Christy nor Hope were interested, and both soon tried to leave. Hope managed to slip away by telling the boys she had to go to the bathroom; now, Christy found herself alone. At that point, Christy has alleged, she was raped by the two football players.

"We never learned about rape in high school," she told a reporter later. "They thought they were protecting us. Do you know what my senior quote in my yearbook was? It says, 'I will trust you until you do something to make me not trust you.' I was just so naïve."

Nationally, more than 3 percent of all female college students have either been the victims of a rape or an attempted rape. In 90 percent of those cases, the assailant was a boyfriend, ex-boyfriend, or classmate of the victim. "College administrators might be disturbed to learn that for every 1,000 women attending their institutions, there may well be 35 incidents of rape in a given academic year," said a report issued by the U.S. Department of Justice. "For a campus with 10,000 women, this would mean the number of rapes could exceed 350. Even more broadly, when projected over the nation's female student population of several million, these figures suggest that rape victimization is a potential problem of large proportion."

The real tragedy behind those statistics is that although it is clear that many young women are potentially the victims of sexual assault, most of them don't realize it. In 2003, when the Gallup Youth Survey asked 1,200 teenagers between the ages of 13 and 17 what they believed was the most important problem facing their generation, just 1 percent said crime. Far more teens were worried about drug abuse, peer pressure, and unemployment than they were about their own safety.

There is no question that dating violence has captured the attention of health professionals as well as law enforcement officials. According to the CDC, the typical victim of "date rape" is a young woman between the ages of 12 and 18 who is assaulted by somebody she knows. One study by the CDC found that some 28 percent of female college students reported being forced into sex

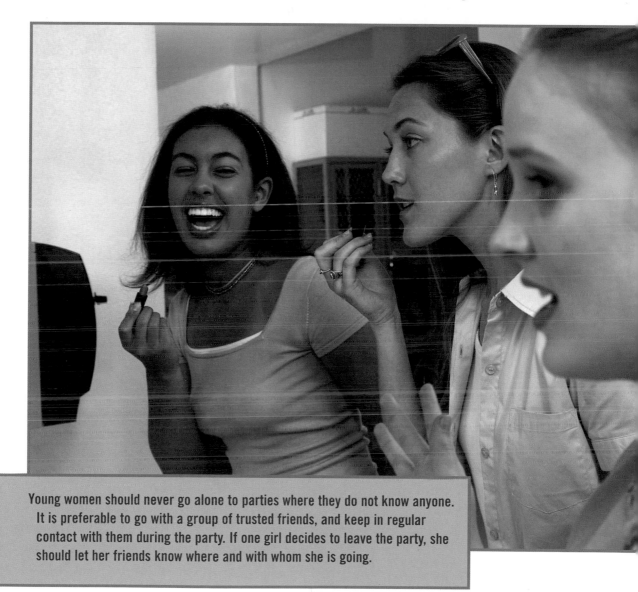

Young women should never go alone to parties where they do not know anyone. It is preferable to go with a group of trusted friends, and keep in regular contact with them during the party. If one girl decides to leave the party, she should let her friends know where and with whom she is going.

at least once since the age of 14. "Only 5 percent of those experiences were reported to police," the CDC wrote. "The term 'hidden rape' has emerged because this survey and many other studies found that sexual assaults are seldom reported to the police."

College students are not the only young people at risk. The CDC reported in 2003 that one out of every ten female high school students is forced to have sexual intercourse when she does not want to. U.S. Department of Justice statistics show that in Alabama, one out of every three rape victims is under the age of 17. In Nebraska, Pennsylvania, and Wisconsin, one in three rape victims is under the age of 16.

The emotional and physical wounds of date rape can be deep and long-lasting. Most rapists do not use condoms or other forms of birth control during the assault. Sexually transmitted diseases can be spread, and there is also the chance that a pregnancy will result from the encounter.

Emotionally, the victim may feel guilt and shame. She may blame herself for being unable to have stopped the assault. She may blame herself for prompting her boyfriend to commit the assault. She may choose to stay in the relationship following the assault, which adds to her confusion and feelings of guilt. The stress may lead to physical symptoms, such as migraine headaches and stomach ailments. She may suffer a loss of concentration, sleeplessness, nightmares, flashbacks, and memory loss. She may come to fear people and be unable to maintain a relationship with another boyfriend.

These are symptoms of Rape Trauma Syndrome, for which there is no quick cure. Only through counseling, support from friends and family members, and the willingness of the victim to put the experience behind her can Rape Trauma Syndrome be overcome. Christy exhibited many symptoms of Rape Trauma Syndrome. After the rape, she rarely left her dorm room for fear of running into her assailants. She started smoking and drinking, then attempted suicide by swallowing an overdose of pills. Eventually, she dropped out of school.

Why Do Teens Rape?

Why are some boys abusive toward their girlfriends? According to the CDC, boys who commit sexual assaults associate with friends who are sexually aggressive; in other words, they talk about sex among themselves and boast to one another about their conquests. To them, dating violence is accepted and expected. Teen members of a group called the Spur Posse were extreme examples of this type of behavior.

The CDC has found that boys who are sexually aggressive prefer to be in control of the date. They initiate the date, demand to do the driving, pick the movie, and pay for the tickets. Most sexually abusive boys drink alcohol and take drugs. At home, they may see the men in their families abuse women. They call their girlfriends constantly to check up on them. They prefer to be in charge of their girlfriends' entire lives, not just on the date—telling her, for example, what she can and cannot do, whom she may have lunch with, who can be her friends. A young man who is abusive may interrogate his girlfriend constantly about where she's been, what she's done, and with whom she's done it with. He may enjoy humiliating and degrading her. He may be very jealous, ready to lash out at the slightest provocation. As incredible as it may sound, many girls stay in these relationships.

Date Rape Drugs

Women who have been date raped may not know they have been raped because they were drugged shortly before the assaults. In recent years, law enforcement officials have tried hard to warn girls about the prevalence of the so-called "date rape drugs," odorless and colorless drugs that can be dissolved in drinks, making the victims unconscious and susceptible to sexual assault. "The victims of this type of crime have problems remembering what exactly happened to them," explains Lieutenant Richard Corriea, head of the sex crimes unit for the San Francisco Police Department. "Women recall having something to drink and then perhaps going outside to smoke or get a breath of fresh air. Then they wake up the next day in a stranger's bed and know something is wrong, but they're not sure what."

"A lot of these rapes go unreported," said Diane E. Gibbons, district attorney of Bucks County in suburban Philadelphia. "The person drinks something and has no idea what occurred. In the cases we've been able to prosecute, someone witnessed the assault

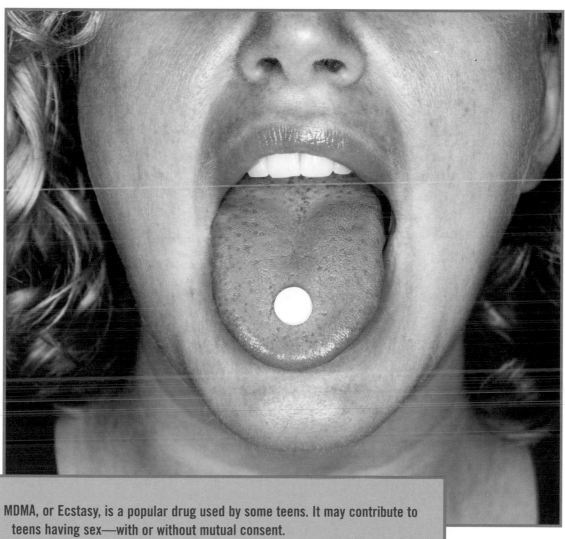

MDMA, or Ecstasy, is a popular drug used by some teens. It may contribute to teens having sex—with or without mutual consent.

and was willing to come forward and help us establish a case." Gibbons helped establish an educational program for female middle-school students that provided them with information on how to recognize a situation in which they might find themselves in danger of date rape.

Drugs that authorities say are used most commonly in sexual assaults include Rohypnol, GHB (Gammahydroxy butyrate), Ketamine, and Ecstasy (MDMA).

Rohypnol, often known as "roofies" and "roaches," comes in white tablets and is a very potent tranquilizer. The effects usually begin within 30 minutes and peak in two hours, although victims may feel the effects of the drug for eight hours or more. Victims may suffer memory impairment, amnesia, drowsiness, diminished eyesight, dizziness, impaired motor skills and judgment, slurred speech, confusion, stomach ailments, and an inability to

THE SPUR POSSE

In 1993, it was common for viewers of daytime television talk shows to see members of the so-called "Spur Posse" chatting about their sexual conquests. The Spur Posse was composed of current and former students at Lakewood High School in a suburb of Los Angeles. Mostly athletes, the posse members took their name from the San Antonio Spurs basketball team, of which they were fans.

They painted a grim picture of teenage sexuality in America. According to the Spur Posse members, each had sex with dozens of female students at Lakewood High. The encounters were usually brief and often in groups. What's more, Spur Posse members assigned a point system to their encounters with the girls, and posse members competed with one another to amass points. One Spur Posse member boasted of scoring 67 points, meaning that he had sex with 67 different girls. "It doesn't count if you have, like, sex with a girl, like 150

urinate. "As insidious, disgusting, and perilous as this may sound, the dangers don't stop there," said Clark Staten, executive director of the Chicago-based Emergency Response and Research Institute. "Besides the worries of unprotected sex, Rohypnol, particularly when mixed with alcohol and other drugs, may lead to respiratory depression, aspiration, and even death. When taken repeatedly, it can lead to physical and psychic dependence, which is thought to increase with both dose and duration of use. An amnesia producing effect of 'roofies' may prevent users from remembering how or why they took the drug or even that they were given it by others. This makes investigation of sexually related or other offenses very difficult and may account for repeated reports of date rapes involving the use of the drug."

Gammahydroxy butyrate, or GHB, is also known as "Georgia Home Boy." GHB comes in powder form. Its effects can hit after

times, 200 times—that's only one point," insisted a Spur Posse member in a television appearance.

Police soon came to believe that some of the liaisons were forced, that Lakewood High girls had been raped by the Spur Posse members. They interviewed several girls and developed cases against nine member of the group. The boys were arrested; however, all but one of the cases fell apart when police determined that the liaisons were consensual. In the one case that went to court, police alleged that a Spur Posse member had sex with a 10-year-old girl. That defendant pleaded guilty and was sentenced to a brief term in a juvenile detention facility. Prosecutors were frustrated by the inability to prosecute most of the cases. Los Angeles Deputy District Attorney Gil Garcetti commented, "We could not prove beyond a reasonable doubt that rape was involved."

15 minutes. In small amounts, it has an effect similar to alcohol, but in larger doses it can cause hallucinations. It can also cause headaches, shaking, spasms, seizures, drowsiness, nausea, irregular heartbeat, and vomiting. Mixed with alcohol, GHB can cause the central nervous system to shut down, which could lead to a loss of consciousness and even death.

Ketamine, known on the street as "Special K, "Vitamin K," or simply "K," comes in liquid, pill, or powder form. Ketamine causes the person to feel as though her mind has become separated from her body. The drug causes amnesia and hallucinations. It also prevents the user from feeling pain and lowers the heart rate, which leads oxygen starvation in the brain. Some victims report temporary paralysis.

MDMA, which stands for methylenedioxymethamphetamine, is most commonly known as Ecstasy. Other nicknames for this drug include Adam, XTC, hug, beans, and the love drug. It causes confusion, depression, sleeplessness, drug craving, anxiety, and paranoia, sometimes weeks after the dose was administered. Victims also exhibit physical symptoms such as muscle tension, involuntary clenching of the jaws, nausea, blurred vision, rapid eye movement, faints, chills, and sweating.

Law enforcement agencies treat people who traffic in date rape drugs no differently from drug dealers who sell cocaine and heroin. In September 2002, federal authorities arrested more than 100 people who were alleged to be selling GHB over the Internet. During the sweep, police in Buffalo, New York, seized more than 750 packages of GHB, shut down three illegal laboratories that were manufacturing the drug, and arrested 35 people.

To guard against drinking a beverage spiked with a date rape drug, girls should never leave their drink unattended. At parties, they should only accept drinks in cans or closed containers. They should never go to a party alone. They should go with friends and keep an eye out for each other. They would do well to listen for talk at the party in which the street names for the drugs are mentioned. If a girl feels ill at a party, she should get help immediately.

Chapter Eight

Parents should take the time to speak with their children about the risks of sexual activity.

What Every Boy and Girl Should Know

"Instruction in social ethics and sexual hygiene must . . . be introduced into the high schools. Most high school pupils are in their earlier period of adolescence. The need for instruction is at no period of life greater than at the threshold of adolescence. The response of the pupil is at no period of life more ready or wholesome. It is, therefore, a matter of greatest importance that instruction in social ethics and sexual hygiene be introduced into all the high schools of the land at the earliest possible day."

Those words were written in 1916 by Dr. Winfield Scott Hall, a professor of medicine at Northwestern University Medical School in Chicago. In the early 20th century Dr. Hall was one of the country's leading experts on sex education. His proposal to teach sex education in the high schools was a radical notion; at the time, sex education was not part of any school's curriculum. It should be noted that while Dr. Hall may have had

approached 200,000 copies. In 1953, Kinsey published a companion volume, *Sexual Behavior in the Human Female*. That book was even more popular, outselling Kinsey's first book.

Meanwhile, in 1954 clinical tests started on the birth control pill. In 1960 the FDA authorized use of the pill for contraceptive purposes. With greater protection from pregnancy, the "sexual revolution" was born as premarital sex became more common.

Although by the 1960s sex education had been introduced in some schools, it was hardly standardized. In many public schools, sex education was incorporated into health education class and taught by gym teachers. When it was time to teach about sex, boys and girls were split into separate classes. It was not unusual for boys to be shown grainy World War II–era movies or filmstrips that had originally been produced to teach soldiers about the dangers of venereal disease. Girls received training on how to use sanitary napkins, or tampons.

In 1966, the National Education Association, the country's largest teachers' union, endorsed a resolution calling for sex education to be taught in U.S. schools. Meanwhile, Wilbur Cohen, undersecretary of what was then known as the Department of Health, Education, and Welfare, issued a report stating that sex education should be a part of every school curriculum and that it should begin in the earliest possible grades.

In the United States, state governments are mostly responsible for what is taught in the schools. By 1980, just six states had made sex education mandatory in their public school districts. A decade later that list had grown to just 16 states and the District of Columbia, although more than 20 states recommended that local school boards establish such programs and just 10 states refused to either mandate or recommend sex education.

As for nonpublic schools, in 1966 the United States Catholic Conference of Bishops created a sex education program for Catholic schools. Those guidelines have been revised over the years. It should be noted that the guidelines issued by the Conference of Bishops are what they are: guidelines. In Catholic schools, sex education is subject to a large degree of local control. As for private Christian schools, most of them are sponsored by local Protestant churches, so their sex education programs often reflect the thinking of the church's leaders.

In recent years sex education has become part of the curriculum in schools throughout the country, with educators concentrating on

Sex-education classes have become common in U.S. schools, and usually include both male and female students.

THE ABSTINENCE-ONLY DEBATE

In 1970, Congress approved a federally subsidized birth control program known as Title X. It was established to help fund family planning clinics operated by state and local governments as well as organizations such as Planned Parenthood. There are about 7,000 such clinics in operation in America. The clinics serve about 4 million women a year, most of them from low-income backgrounds. In addition to obtaining birth control at the clinics, the women also receive gynecological examinations, blood pressure evaluations, pelvic examinations, breast examinations, and Pap tests, which screen for cervical cancer. The women are also tested for AIDS and other sexually transmitted diseases.

Many women also go to the clinics for contraceptive services. It is believed that since Title X funding became available, federal funds have helped women avoid more than 20 million pregnancies, including more than 5 million pregnancies by teenagers.

Congress gives about $275 million a year in Title X funding. Proponents of the program argue that this is money well spent: if Title X did not exist, proponents say, those 20 million pregnancies would have resulted in babies born to mothers who could not afford them, requiring taxpayers to provide increased welfare payments and other support to the mothers and their children. Title X proponents argue that those expenses would have cost far more than the $275 million a year the federal government allots to the clinics.

Beginning in 1981, Title X appropriations included money for programs to encourage "chastity and self-discipline" among teenagers. At first, the money provided for a small public education program designed to encourage abstinence, but by the late 1990s, conservative lawmakers in Washington were able to greatly expand abstinence education, winning funding that totaled more than $100 million. This money was earmarked for schools that would establish abstinence-only programs in sex education classes. Most state governments accepted the money, passing it on to schools that agreed to the government restrictions on the money.

To obtain the money, schools as well as other organizations with abstinence-only sex education programs must emphasize in their classrooms that abstinence is the only sure way to avoid sexually transmitted diseases and unwanted pregnancies. Indeed, the only allowable way to discuss contraception in such classes is in the context of how it fails. As reported by the Kaiser Family Foundation study, a third of public school sex education classes stress abstinence. "We never discuss where to get birth control or anything like that. We can't," Kelli Lehew, a sex education teacher at a Maryland YMCA, told a reporter. "We do tell them that birth control is ineffective."

In 2002, President George W. Bush proposed an increase in the money available to abstinence-only sex education classes. "My administration will elevate abstinence education from an afterthought to an urgent goal," Bush insisted. "We should spend at least as much each year on promoting the conscience of our children as we do on providing them with contraception.".

Bush asked Congress to hike spending for abstinence-only education to $135 million a year. Congress eventually approved an increase of $15 million; nevertheless, the message was clear: the federal government now believed in abstinence-only education. This was a far different attitude than what Surgeon General Jocelyn Elders had advocated just a decade before—that condoms should be available to help young people avoid sexually transmitted diseases and unwanted pregnancies.

Many health professionals oppose abstinence-only education. Sarah Brown, head of the National Campaign to Prevent Teen Pregnancy, says teenage birth rates have been falling for two reasons: more teens are abstaining from sex, and more teens are also practicing contraception.

Even Dr. David Stacher, Bush's former surgeon general, questioned whether abstinence-only education is sufficient. In 2001, he issued a report urging that sex education go beyond just delivering an abstinence-only message. "Every child needs to have equity of opportunity for sex education," said Dr. Stacher. "That's the point we are trying to make."

such issues as sexually transmitted diseases, abstinence, and contraception. "Today, virtually all public schools provide some form of sex education," said a 2000 report on the state of sex education in the United States commissioned by the Kaiser Family Foundation. "Sex education is in fact so prominent in the lives of young people that it is now a primary source of information on sexual health issues."

The Kaiser study found that 89 percent of all public school students between the seventh and twelfth grades are exposed to some form of sex education in school. They learn about abstinence, STDs, and the basics of reproduction. Some students also receive education on tangential issues, such as how to deal with pressure from their boyfriends or girlfriends to have sex, the emotional consequences of maintaining a sexual relationship, how to talk to their parents or partners about sexual health issues, how to obtain tests for STDs, and how to obtain contraceptives. The Kaiser study found that two-thirds of the schools in the United States that provide sex education offer a comprehensive program that gives information on abstinence and how to obtain birth control, while a third of the schools emphasize abstinence as the only option for avoiding pregnancy and sexually transmitted diseases. In recent years, the administration of President George W. Bush proposed an increase in federal funding for sex education programs to schools that offer abstinence-only sex education classes.

Polls conducted by the Gallup Youth Survey support the findings of the Kaiser Family Foundation study. In 2001, the Gallup Organization asked 501 young people to identify the topics that are covered in their health education classes. A total of 90 percent of them said they have covered AIDS, 81 percent said they have received information about other sexually transmitted diseases, 85 percent said they discussed teen pregnancy, 77 percent said they received information about abstaining from sex until marriage, 69 percent said their courses covered birth control, and 68 percent said the issue of abortion was covered in their classes. Other topics covered in health education classes included drug and alcohol abuse, cigarette smoking, chewing tobacco, steroid use, nutrition, exercise, eating disorders, the effects of loud music on hearing, and the importance of getting enough sleep.

For the most part, students seem satisfied with what they are being taught in sex education class. "Overall, students give mostly As and Bs in terms of how well their sex education is preparing them to understand the

Students who have had sex education may feel more prepared to make decisions about sex. Although teens who choose to abstain from sex agree that the decision is difficult, many are happy and satisfied with their decision to wait.

basics of reproduction, waiting to have sex, and dealing with the pressure to have sex," the Kaiser study said. "Students rate the teaching of communication skills—such as how to talk with their parents or a boyfriend or a girlfriend—somewhat lower. Instruction in how to use and where to get birth control—due in part to the fact that many courses do not teach this—also gets lower grades from students." Students who said they had sex edu-

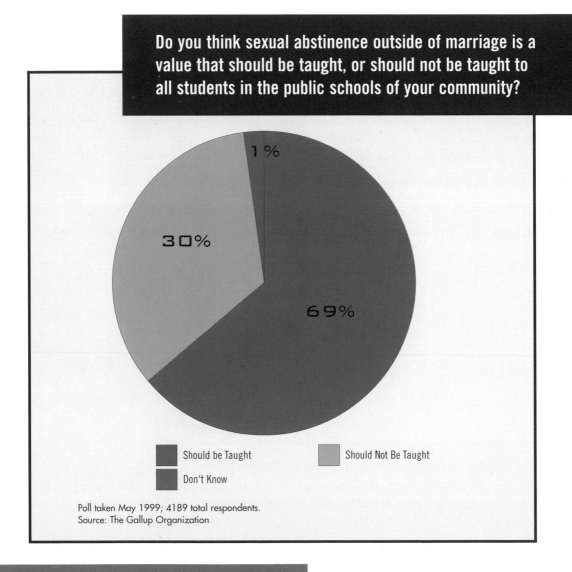

Do you think sexual abstinence outside of marriage is a value that should be taught, or should not be taught to all students in the public schools of your community?

1%

30%

69%

Should be Taught   Should Not Be Taught

Don't Know

Poll taken May 1999; 4189 total respondents.
Source: The Gallup Organization

cation in school reported feeling more prepared to make decisions about sex — including the decision to abstain — than students who said they had no sex education.

Today, sex education classes are largely coeducational and focus on biological, emotional, and practical issues. The Kaiser study found that most sex education teachers in U.S. schools have received training in the area and have been teaching sex education for five years or more. Few sex education teachers spend all their time entirely on sex education, but more than half of the people teaching sex education are full-time health teachers. Others typically teach biology or the physical sciences, home economics, or family and consumer science. Just 14 percent are physical education teachers.

All schools that provide sex education focus on helping students make intelligent choices. The Kaiser report said, "What are the actual messages of sex education in pubic secondary schools today? Students, teachers, and principals nationwide report that the large majority of sex education courses stress a comprehensive message, teaching that young people should wait to have sex, but if they don't they should use birth control and practice safer sex."

Glossary

AMNESIA—Partial or total loss of memory caused by shock, brain injury, or illness.

ANXIETY—Mental condition characterized by a feeling of powerlessness to cope with threatening events, often accompanied by such physical effects as sweating and trembling.

CEREBRAL PALSY—Disorder resulting from damage to the central nervous system, usually characterized by mobility problems.

CERVIX—The lower, neck-like portion of the uterus that protrudes into the vagina. The cervix contains a tiny opening; during labor, the opening widens, permitting passage of the baby.

DEPRESSION—Emotional condition characterized by feelings of sadness, hopelessness, and inadequacy.

DYSLEXIA—Difficulty in reading, often characterized by transposition of letters, often caused by a genetic defect or brain injury.

INTRAVENOUS—Method of introducing a drug into the body through a vein.

LATEX—Synthetic rubber used in the manufacture of many products, including condoms.

LIBERTINE—Person who leads an unrestrained, sexually active life.

LICENTIOUS—Morally unrestrained, particularly in sexual conduct.

OBSTETRICIAN—Physician who specializes in the care of pregnant women; most babies born in hospitals are delivered by obstetricians.

OVULATION—Process is which a mature ovum becomes ready to accept sperm.

PARANOIA—Mental disorder characterized by delusions or feelings of persecution.

Glossary

PROPHYLACTIC—Any device, medication, or treatment that guards against disease; condoms are also known as prophylactics.

TRANQUILIZER—Medication administered to control anxiety and other mental disorders.

TRANSGENDER—Lifestyle in which gender lines are blurred; usually refers to men who dress as women.

URETHRA—In men, the canal that discharges urine and semen.

UTERUS—Hollow organ in which the ovum develops into an embryo and fetus.

Internet Resources

http://www.gallup.com

The Gallup Organization's World Wide Web page features information on the Gallup Youth Surveys as well as the other polling work conducted by the organization.

http://www.gallup.com/poll/analyses/educaYouth/

This is the Gallup Organization's direct link to articles and poll results covering education and youth issues.

http://www.cdc.gov

The Centers for Disease Control and Prevention makes available on its Internet site dozens of studies and articles about teen sexuality and its consequences.

http://www.kff.org

The Henry J. Kaiser Foundation's study, "Sex Education in America," can be downloaded at the organization's Internet home page. The web site also includes other studies on public health and sexuality issues.

http://www.nrlc.org
http://www.naral.org

The two sides of the abortion debate are examined at the World Wide Web sites maintained by the National Right to Life Committee and NARAL (National Abortion and Reproductive Rights Action League) Pro-Choice America.

http://www.teenpregnancy.org

The National Campaign to Prevent Teen Pregnancy maintains a World Wide Web site that includes a number of statistics, news reports, studies, and other resources that examine the issue of teen pregnancy.

http://www.advocatesforyouth.org

The Washington-based organization, formerly known as the Center for Population Options, maintains a World Wide Web site designed to help young people make responsible decisions about their sexual health.

Internet Resources

http://www.hrw.org

The report "Hatred in the Hallways: Violence and Discrimination Against Lesbian, Gay and Transgender Students in U.S. Schools," can be downloaded at the World Wide Web site maintained by Human Rights Watch.

http://www.siecus.org

The World Wide Web page of the Sexuality Information and Education Council of the United States contains information on many issues related to teens and sex. A "For Teens" section lists hotlines for teens to call when they have questions about contraception, sexually transmitted diseases, abuse, and gay issues.

http://www.parentstv.org

The Parents Television Council rates television programs to determine those suitable for young viewers.

http://www.mediascope.org/index_old.htm

The California-based nonprofit organization Mediascope studies issues affecting young people and the entertainment industry, including sexuality, obesity, school violence, and substance abuse.

http://www.guttmacher.org

The Alan Guttmacher Institute was founded by the late Dr. Alan Guttmacher, an obstetrician and gynecologist who served as president of Planned Parenthood. The organization has studied dozens of sexuality issues, many of which involve young people.

Further Reading

Bell, Ruth, et al. *Changing Bodies, Changing Lives: A Book for Teens on Sex and Relationships*. New York: Times Books, 1998.

Bender, David L., and Bruno Leone, eds. *Teenage Sexuality: Opposing Viewpoints.* San Diego: Greenhaven Press, 1994.

Eller, T. Suzanne, editor. *Real Teens, Real Stories, Real Life.* Tulsa, Okla.: River Oak Publishing, 2002.

Immell, Myra, editor. *Teen Pregnancy*. San Diego: Greenhaven Press, 2001.

Meeker, Meg. *Epidemic: How Teen Sex is Killing our Kids*. Washington, D.C.: LifeLine Press, 2002.

Thompson, Sharon. *Going All the Way: Teenage Girls' Tales of Sex, Romance and Pregnancy.* New York: Hill and Wang, 1995.

Index

abortion, 9, 16, 35–41, 42, 99
Abortion Control Act (Pennsylvania),
   38–39
abstinence, 18–19, **22**, 24, **32**, 33,
   96–99, **100**, 101
   See also sex education
abuse, child, **20**, 21
adoption, 9, 16, 35, 41–43
Advocates for Youth, 75, 76–77
aggression, **82**, 83–84
AIDS, 12, 19, 26, **29**, **44**, 45–46,
   48–50, 52–53, 75–77, 96, 98
   See also sexually transmitted diseases
   (STDs)
Alan Guttmacher Institute, 18, 39–40
alcohol, **17**, 20, 28, 77
American Enterprise Institute, 28–29
Ashe, Arthur, 53
   See also AIDS

Besharov, Douglas J., 28–29
birth control pills, 24, **26**, 27, 30, 32, 94
   See also contraceptives
birth defects, 21
   See also pregnancy
Brown, Sarah, 19, 97
   See also National Campaign to Prevent
   Teen Pregnancy
Bush, George W., 19, 97, 98

Carnegie Council, 12
CDC. *See* U.S. Centers for Disease Control
   and Prevention (CDC)
cervical cap, 31
   See also contraceptives
chancroids, 50
   See also sexually transmitted diseases

(STDs)
ChildTrends, **42**
chlamydia trachomatis, 48, 50, 51
   See also sexually transmitted diseases
   (STDs)
Cohen, Wilbur, 94
condoms, 23–28, **29**, 30, 32, 48–49, 53
   See also contraceptives
contraceptives, 12, 16, 23–33, **47**, 58,
   83, 96–99, 100
   failure rates, 32
   See also pregnancy
Corriea, Richard, 84–85
Corrozza, Carol, 27
cytomegalovirus (CMV), 50
   See also sexually transmitted diseases
   (STDs)

date rape. *See* rape
date rape drugs, 84–89
   See also rape
Depo-Provera, 30–31
   See also contraceptives
desensitization, 63–64
   See also media
diaphragm, 31, **32**
   See also contraceptives
discretionary activities, teen, 12
drugs, **17**, 20, 28, **76**, 77
date rape, 84–89

Ecstasy (MDMA), **85**, 86, 88
   See also date rape drugs
education, 16–17, 18–19
   See also sex education
Elders, Jocelyn, 24, 97
emergency contraceptive (EC), 33

Numbers in **bold italic** refer to captions or graphs.

Index

Index

Index

Picture Credits

Contributors

GEORGE GALLUP JR. is chairman of The George H. Gallup International Institute (sponsored by The Gallup International Research and Education Center, or GIREC) and is senior scientist and member of the GIREC council. Mr. Gallup serves as chairman of the board of the National Coalition for Children's Justice and as a trustee of the National Fatherhood Initiative. He serves on many other boards in the area of health, education and religion.

Mr. Gallup is recognized internationally for his research and study on youth, health, religion, and urban problems. He has written numerous books including *My Kids On Drugs?* with Art Linkletter (Standard, 1981), *The Great American Success Story* with Alec Gallup and William Proctor (Dow Jones-Irwin, 1986), *Growing Up Scared in America* with Wendy Plump (Morehouse, 1995), *Surveying the Religious Landscape: Trends in U.S. Beliefs* with D. Michael Lindsay (Morehouse, 1999), and *The Next American Spirituality* with Timothy Jones (Chariot Victor Publishing, 1999).

Mr. Gallup received his BA degree from the Princeton University Department of Religion in 1954, and holds seven honorary degrees. He has received many awards, including the Charles E. Wilson Award in 1994, the Judge Issacs Lifetime Achievement Award in 1996, and the Bethune-DuBois Institute Award in 2000. Mr. Gallup lives near Princeton, New Jersey, with his wife, Kingsley. They have three grown children.

THE GALLUP YOUTH SURVEY was founded in 1977 by Dr. George Gallup to provide ongoing information on the opinions, beliefs and activities of America's high school students and to help society meet its responsibility to youth. The topics examined by the Gallup Youth Survey have covered a wide range— from abortion to zoology. From its founding through the year 2001, the Gallup Youth Survey sent more than 1,200 weekly reports to the Associated Press, to be distributed to newspapers around the nation. Since January 2002, Gallup Youth Survey reports have been made available on a weekly basis through the Gallup Tuesday Briefing.

HAL MARCOVITZ is a Pennsylvania-based journalist. His other titles in the GALLUP YOUTH SURVEY series include *Teens and Suicide*, *Teens and Race*, and *Teens and Family Issues*. He lives in Chalfont, Pennsylvania, with his wife, Gail, and daughters Ashley and Michelle.